Contents

CONTENTS

IV. POLISH-AMERICAN RELATIONS IN THE 1990s

V. POLAND'S NATIONAL SECURITY PROGRAM

VI. DEVELOPMENTS IN THE MID-1990s

THE PRESIDENCY
AND GOVERNANCE
IN POLAND

Yesterday and Today

Edited by

Kenneth W. Thompson

Volume X
In the Miller Center Series on
A World in Change

UNIVERSITY
PRESS OF
AMERICA

Lanham • New York • Oxford

The Miller Center

University of Virginia

Copyright © 1997 by
University Press of America,® Inc.
4720 Boston Way
Lanham, Maryland 20706

12 Hid's Copse Rd.
Cummor Hill, Oxford OX2 9JJ

Copublished by arrangement with
The Miller Center of Public Affairs,
University of Virginia

The views expressed by the author(s) of this publication do not necessarily represent the opinions of the Miller Center. We hold to Jefferson's dictum that: "Truth is the proper and sufficient antagonist to error, and has nothing to fear from the conflict, unless by human interposition, disarmed of her natural weapons, free argument and debate."

Library of Congress Cataloging-in-Publication Data

The presidency and governance in Poland : yesterday and today / edited by Kenneth W. Thompson.
p. cm.--(Miller Center series on a world in change ; v. 10
1. Poland--Politics and government--1989- 2. Post-communism--Poland. 3. Presidents--Poland. 4. Constitutional history--Poland. 5. Poland--Relations-- United States. 6. United States--Relations--Poland. 7. National security-- Poland. I. Thompson, Kenneth W. II. Series.
DK4449.P74 1997 943.805'7--dc21 97-27416 CIP

ISBN: 0-7618-0870-1 (cloth: alk. ppr.)
ISBN: 0-7618-0871-X (pbk: alk. ppr.)

TO
LADY BLANKA ROSENSTIEL

WHOSE GENEROSITY MAKES POSSIBLE
THE MILLER CENTER'S PROGRAM
ON GOVERNANCE IN POLAND

Preface

Poland's experiment in postwar democracy has attracted attention worldwide. Some ask in tones that recall Lincoln, "Can this republic long endure?" Another more hopeful refrain often heard is, "If Poland can't make it, who can?" referring to the states of eastern and central Europe and the former Soviet republics. Yet a cloud of uncertainty hangs over even the Polish experiment. At certain times the sun breaks through, as with Solidarity and Lech Walesa, but clouds return and friends are disheartened by particular elections or the presence of former Communists in portions of authority. Then Poland moves ahead, reflecting the talents and resolve of the Polish people.

We should remind ourselves that the future of the American republic was in doubt in 1776, 1789, 1812, 1861, 1864, 1917, 1933, 1941, and 1947. In every era, journalists and politicians sounded the alarm. In the Cold War, the United States and the Soviet Union were hegemonic powers. We have been the world's sole remaining superpower only once. In times of crisis, U.S. leaders have echoed Lincoln's anguish over this country's survival. We need to remember that America's dominance has not characterized the long sweep of modern history. Americans have risen to meet historic challenges. Our moments of greatness more often than not have coincided with the appearance of threats looming on the horizon.

Perhaps we shall be better able to understand Poland's often painful and difficult historical course if we reflect on the long line of crises and perils faced by Americans and overcome. Remembering out own past may help us to better understand the present challenges facing others. With all of their differences, the United States and Poland have learned what it means to live in a changing world.

vii

Introduction

Poland has grown in importance for the United States in the 20th century, perhaps because of the ever-changing patterns of the world crisis. Four times partitioned and overrun by the armies of Germany and Russia, Poland has suffered unspeakable carnage and human devastation from the major conflicts in the west. It has been partitioned and has lost its freedom. One of the worst nightmares that haunts every sensitive conscience is the world's collective memories of the thousands of Poles trapped and killed in the Warsaw Uprising. Try as we will, none but the most inhumane can forget the barbarism of the final days of the war and Stalin's hard-hearted refusal to allow Americans to come to the aid of the victims.

Once again, Poland has risen from the ashes. Its story is a heroic chapter in the history of the human race. In chapter one of *The Presidency and Governance in Poland,* a retired American official and an expert on local government help the reader understand Poland's recovery and why it should matter to the world. Gifford Malone is a retired foreign service officer who rose to the rank of minister counselor. He has been a generous friend of the Miller Center virtually from its creation. The son of the greatest of Jeffersonian historians and biographers, Dumas Malone, Gifford earned credentials as a highly regarded expert on the Soviet Union and Eastern Europe. He is the founding president of the American Committee for Aid to Poland. Clay Wirt is the executive secretary of the Virginia Local Government Management Association and legislative counsel and deputy director of the Virginia Municipal League. Proceeding from different vantage points, Malone and Wirt in the first section of the book trace Poland's postwar and post-Communist history and development. They confront many of the recurrent questions that people ask about Poland. They help to put in context the concern most Americans have about former

Communists in the government. They trace the impressive growth of Poland's Gross Domestic Product (GDP). They do not hesitate to point to weaknesses and problems, for example, in sectors of local government. Malone and Wirt are basically optimistic, however, about Poland's future.

Another longtime friend of the Miller Center is Polish professor and Supreme Court Justice Leszek Garlicki. On questions of constitutionalism and elections, he has been a tutor to all of us. Widely respected internationally as a law professor at the University of Warsaw, he has lectured and taught at universities in the United States, including the University of Indiana, the Law and Graduate Center at Capital University in Ohio, and the University of California. He visited the Miller Center in 1990, 1992, and 1993 and continues to advise us on developments in Poland. In 1992, he discussed the Walesa presidency and the parliamentary elections and argued that the popular conception of the elections having been a total victory for the Left is false. He traces the origin of the modern Polish presidency going back to Józef Piłsudski and the rebirth of Poland in 1918. The 1921 Constitution provided for a weak presidency and was drafted to limit strong leaders such as Piłsudski, even though the latter did not seek the presidency then. The 1935 Constitution offered the chance for a strong presidency, but in April 1935, Piłsudski died of cancer, and no one else had the qualities required by that Constitution. With the 1952 Constitution, the Communist Party grasped power and managed to hold it for 38 years. As a result of compromises between the Solidarity trade union and the Communist Party, a stronger presidency emerged. By 1990, the Communist Party had disappeared and a split developed within Solidarity. The new president was to be elected by popular vote. Walesa won, but with the division in Solidarity, his support was less than had been forecast. Garlicki analyzes in depth the relation between the president and the parliament and the uncertainty of party support for the presidency. Walesa was unable to build a powerful political party of his own. Garlicki's essay illustrates constitutional and political change in Poland.

The author of chapter three considers political, social, and economic developments and dilemmas in Poland. Maciej Kozlowski is the deputy chief of mission of the Polish embassy in Washington.

His approach is multifaceted. He reviews the transition from communism to democracy, which is part of a wider change in the former Soviet Union and Eastern Europe that involves one-third of the world's population. Kozlowski compares east Germany with Poland and points out the advantages of the latter but also some of its most persistent problems. He deals with unemployment, inflation, and differences between urban and rural areas, putting special emphasis on the psychological problems brought about by change. He singles out one especially urgent problem: how to deal with the functionaries of the previous regime. This and other transition problems are complex and difficult, as the Polish official makes clear.

Part III returns to a theme that strikes a familiar note in Polish history, namely, constitutional change. The contributors relate this theme to political change reflected in the 1993 elections. The elections inevitably determine the effectiveness of the executive. In the first essay in this section, Professor Garlicki revisits the constitutions of 1921, 1935, and 1952. What each constitution provided for was not necessarily realized. The absence of an available strong president was as important as the constitutional provisions. For example, the 1935 Constitution provided for a strong presidency, but by then the strongest candidate, Piłsudski, was dead. As for the 1952 Constitution, the first secretary of the Communist Party headed the government and was in effect both head of state and head of government. Constitutional texts and personal behavior were not always compatible. The Communists found it convenient to adopt the constitution of 1952 and fashion it to their ends. Garlicki examines at length the relation of presidents to the parliament and the cabinet. Over the period from 1989 to 1993, the changes and modification of constitutional relations are the subject of extended analysis.

Finally, Garlicki examines the 1993 elections and asks the question, who won and who lost. Only one right-wing party had enough votes to gain seats in the *Sejm*, and it was the Confederation for an Independent Poland. The new Nazi party failed to gain seats of its own. The Left won the election, and the Democratic Union Party, although it gained 74 seats in parliament, in effect lost. At first glance, the Communists appeared to win, but

Garlicki questions their victory, given their identification with Cold War Communists. The overall situation is far more complex; it deserves extended treatment. The answer Garlicki appears to give is that only time will tell who won and who lost.

A second view of the 1993 elections is by Washington and Lee Professor Krzysztof Jasiewicz, whom some call the Theodore White of Polish presidential and parliamentary politics. He has written on the parliamentary elections of 1985, 1989, and 1990 (presidential) and 1991. He calls attention to some of the peculiarities of the new Polish electoral law that can transform a moderate victory in number of votes into a massive victory in seats. There are various ways of looking at the election, and they lead to different results. Whichever method is used, the post-Communist Left appears to be the victor for now, and Professor Jasiewicz explains why this victory occurred. Part of their strength was their success in presenting themselves as champions of that part of the population who saw themselves threatened by economic reform, such as pensioners, teachers, and health service workers. He proposes seven "fathers" who influenced the electoral trends in the direction they occurred. Along the way he takes a more favorable view of the Democratic Union Party's situation than Garlicki's view. He identifies the midwife of the post-Communist victory as a doctor of medicine and Catholic fundamentalist, Bogumita Boba, who resisted the creation of a coalition that might have helped groups such as the Democratic Union. Her attitude toward politics was especially costly to the moderates.

Part IV takes up the question of Polish-American relations in the 1990s. Dr. Bogusław Winid from the Polish embassy addresses this question. He is both a scholar and a diplomat. He first discusses Polish-American relations in the interwar period from 1919 to 1939. Next he reviews Polish attitudes today toward NATO membership and the Partnership for Peace (PFP) initiative. Some of us remember hearing about the efforts of the great Polish pianist and leader Ignacy Paderewski during and after World War I to gain support for Poland. The Dawes Plan in 1924 gave Poland new possibilities for assistance. The Stabilization Plan and Loan of 1927 introduced still other possibilities. Problems arose later that operated against Poland. The discussion of the period beginning in 1924 is familiar to some present-day Americans.

Part V throws the spotlight on the transformation process in Poland. Minister Counsellor Kozlowski returned to the Miller Center to discuss Poland's national security program. The discussion was held against the background of the 50th anniversary of the 1944 Warsaw Uprising against the Nazi occupation.

In speaking of the 50th anniversary celebration, Kozlowski praised President Lech Walesa for making it "an international event of reconciliation," contrasting it with the Normandy reunion where only the victorious allies celebrated D-Day. He contrasts the attitudes expressed by the new president of Germany, Roman Herzog, with those of President Yeltsin, who sent his chief of staff. Vice President Gore represented the United States, and Prime Minister John Major represented the British. As a result, the reconciliation that took place between Poland and Germany did not develop between Poland and Russia. The remainder of Kozlowski's presentation focused on the current security situation in Europe, which he described as unclear. The Polish people feared the possible revival of the Russian empire and the effect it would have on Poland and neighboring countries. Poland is seeking an insurance policy and is turning to NATO. Kozlowski worries about the grey space between NATO and Russia and sees the solution in Poland's membership in NATO.

Gifford Malone and Clay Wirt returned to the Miller Center on 6 June 1995 to review and summarize developments in present-day Poland through the mid-1990s. Both continue to be optimistic about the future of Poland. Each points to some of the more stubborn and continuing problems. Each rehearses some of the favorable and unfavorable developments in Poland in 1995. Among the positive developments are a 5 percent growth rate of the GDP, a private sector contribution to GDP of 56 percent coupled with strong exports, keeping the deficit under control, and a rising standard of living. Negative developments, however, continue as high unemployment, low agricultural production, poor labor mobility, inadequate housing, and a 40 percent drop in the standard of living since economic reforms went into effect. Decentralization of government is an issue, as in the involvement of former

Communists in government, including party organization. Malone in particular offers a tour d'horizon of all of the problems facing the government. For his part Wirt evaluates the Manager to Manager Program of city managers in the two countries and the funding it has attracted. School systems in the United States continue exchanges with Polish school systems. One encouraging aspect of exchanges is the extension of the stays of visitors to Poland and the United States. While Poland has its problems, there is significant positive movement, and the two Americans take heart in those developments as a portent of the future.

I.

THE IMPORTANCE
OF POLAND TO AMERICANS

CHAPTER ONE

Poland: 1992*

GIFFORD D. MALONE AND CLAY L. WIRT

NARRATOR: Gifford Dumas Malone is a retired State Department officer and minister counselor in the Foreign Service. He has also held high positions in the United States Information Agency. He is currently president of the American Committee for Aid to Poland. He chairs meetings of the private sector group involved in assisting Poland, and spent most of his career in Soviet and East European affairs. He served in the American Embassy in Moscow and twice in the American Embassy in Poland, the second time heading the political section.

From a selfish standpoint, the Miller Center is especially proud that we were able to publish his book, *Political Advocacy and Cultural Communication: Organizing the Nation's Public Diplomacy*, which is certainly one of the best studies of public diplomacy. He also has the lead chapter entitled "Public Diplomacy: Organizing for the Future," in a book called *The Stanton Report Revisited*.

Clay Wirt is a friend of more recent origin, but someone whose work we have come to respect. He is the executive secretary of the Virginia Local Government Management Association and legislative counsel and deputy director of the Virginia Municipal League. He is a member of the Virginia Bar, having received his law degree from Georgetown University with a specialty in international law. In an earlier incarnation, he was elected county supervisor in Johnson County, Kansas, and served for two years as

---

*Presented in a Forum at the Miller Center of Public Affairs on 1 April 1992.

chairman of the Johnson County Board of Supervisors. He has been an assistant to Senator Bob Dole.

We are delighted that we have two such well-informed and productive members of our Miller Center family concerned with Poland. They represent the millions of Americans for whom Poland's future is a deep and abiding interest.

MR. MALONE: Ken has told you about my personal background, which probably explains some of my biases with respect to Poland. I was also diplomat-in-residence here at the University of Virginia for one year and during that year and the following year taught a course on Poland and the Soviet Union. In these ways, I have become fairly deeply involved with Poland and the Polish people.

When I lived in Poland as a Foreign Service officer, I never thought I would see the day when the things we hoped would happen did happen. Most other people did not foresee it either. I thought some day the Poles would emerge from their ordeal, but that it would be a long time in coming. Of course, it all happened rapidly.

I believe that what happens in Poland is tremendously impor-tant, and that is why I am involved with the American Committee for Aid to Poland (ACAP). I believe that the United States and the West in general have a stake in Poland's future. What happens politically and economically is important to us. Poland is a strategic interest, too, because it is a country of 38 million people in the heart of Europe, and one would hate to see it become authoritarian, nondemocratic, or lapse into chaos. Events occurring in Poland are also important for the countries of the former Soviet Union.

I often visit Warsaw, and I usually try to call on certain members of parliament whom I know. One of them is Professor Geremek, one of the leaders of the Democratic Union and a wise man. Professor Geremek and I were talking in January 1992 about whether the American public was losing interest in Poland because of the events in the Soviet Union. I told him that in a policy sense, I did not think we were. Recent events in the former Soviet Union made it more important that Poland succeed. He told me that he had been talking to President Yeltsin in Moscow and Yeltsin had said, "If you Poles don't make it, there isn't any hope for the rest of us." That comment is worth pondering.

I want to consider what seems to be happening in Poland now, although with the caveat that I have not been there since January of 1992 and things change fast in that country. Certainly the basic problem is the economic issue. The transformation of the country to a market economy is enormously difficult. Everyone knows that, but when people see the progress as I do each time I go back, they are always struck by the advances. It has become a cliche to say that no one has ever done it before, but it is true that no one ever has, and there is not any blueprint. The Poles are getting a lot of advice on the subject, but what they are doing and trying to do is extremely difficult. There are enormous problems.

I sometimes think that in looking at these problems, people forget how much Poland has accomplished in two years. This radical transformation of the economy started in January 1990. The so-called shock therapy has run into trouble, but they have nevertheless accomplished a great deal.

Every time I return to Warsaw, the city looks a little different. The private stores are springing up as well as all kinds of private enterprise. Queues no longer exist. The stores carry virtually anything anyone wants. It costs a great deal, which is the downside.

Political changes are also noteworthy. When I first returned to Poland in June 1990 after an 18-year absence, everyone was talking about a meeting that had just occurred in the Central Committee of Solidarity in which various members had been criticizing one another. They thought this internal criticism was shocking, terrible, and surprising. It was understandable, of course, since Solidarity had been an umbrella organization held together largely by common opposition to the Communist regime. They were so new to politics at that time, however, that this type of disagreement seemed strange and even frightening. Now the political situation has evolved far beyond that stage.

They are progressing economically, despite the problems. The private sector now accounts for about 40 to 50 percent of Gross Domestic Product (GDP) in Poland, which is quite a lot. It may indeed account for even more, because, understandably, a good deal of private activity is not reported for tax reasons. I was also told in

January that 70,000 private sector jobs a month were being added to the economy, which is quite impressive. According to Polish statistics issued in March 1992, private sector industrial production increased by about 25 percent in 1991. The downside is that the public sector lost more jobs than the private sector gained, and industrial production in the public sector decreased about 12 percent last year.

The problem is, how do you privatize an economy like this one? How do you convert from state-owned to privately owned enterprises? The kind of private enterprise that is springing up is perhaps not quite spontaneous, but almost so. The problem of how you deal with the huge, inefficient, unprofitable, grossly overstaffed state enterprises still has not been solved. Other countries—Czechoslovakia and Hungary—are also trying to deal with this question in different ways. It is an enormous problem.

Social costs come with the economic transition. Unemployment is about 12 percent. About 2.2 million people are out of work, and that number is expected to rise by the end of this year to about 3.5 million. Living standards are lower than they were two or three years ago, but those standards, of course, are hard to measure. You cannot consider only inflation or examine statistics because many things that were not available two or three years ago are now available. Nevertheless, people feel that living standards are down. They are in a period of austerity in a country which has faced austerity for a long time. The government recently cut pensions, for example, to save money. It also stopped giving money to a lot of local institutions that provide social services for people.

At the same time, trade unions are pushing the government to ease the austerity program, and agricultural interests want to continue and even expand subsidies. These social costs are reflected in politics, as the elections for the parliament that took place last October demonstrated. The election results reflected the popular dissatisfaction. The Polish Parliament now has 29 parties. The one that has the largest number of seats has a little over 12 percent, and the rest are smaller and scattered. The people who were running for office at that time made all kinds of promises, naturally, which now they are unable to keep.

6

It took nearly three months of discussion in parliament to form a government. Now they are arguing about economic reform. The ruling coalition, led by Mr. Olszewski, the prime minister, is shaky, and it is unclear how they are going to deal with this problem. In April, parliament will renew discussions on the government's economic plan, having rejected it last month. We will see what happens. In crude terms, politics is threatening the economic reform program. Other political questions, too, are worrisome.

The trouble in parliament is not just due to economics. A great deal of difficulty is involved in reaching agreements and forming coalitions. Politically, compromise is not a concept that has been well understood in the past.

Hopefully, the fact that 29 political parties are present does not indicate the revival of a historic problem. Nevertheless, one recalls that in the 17th and 18th centuries, the Polish republic, which had an elected king, became weaker and weaker, because none of the nobility could agree, and each one had the right to veto (the *liberum* veto).

After 123 years of partition, Poland almost miraculously put itself back together following World War I. With the vast number of parties that then emerged, however, things became so chaotic that Marshal Piłsudski carried out a coup d'etat against the elected government. I am not suggesting that President Walesa is about to launch a coup, but there are problems in building democracies. It is natural that problems should arise, but it is nevertheless something that should concern people.

Local government is also just beginning. In the spring of 1990, 50,000 new local government officials were elected. You can imagine how difficult it is to solve local problems without any experience.

Even though my discussion has focused on the problems that are occurring, I tend to be optimistic for the long term. The Poles I deal with in Warsaw and the politicians that I see tend to agree, which is heartening. Plenty of problems exist, however. The West can and has already helped address these problems in important ways. It helped with the critical stabilization of the Polish currency. Largely under the leadership of the United States, Poland has reduced its debt. Technical assistance has also been provided in

7

various ways. For instance, the Polish-American Enterprise Fund helps small businesses get started in Poland.

I attended a conference last June sponsored by the Institute for East-West Security Studies in Bardejov, Slovakia, in which many Poles, Czechs, Slovaks, and Hungarians participated. Interestingly, they all agreed on what the West should be doing. They said they needed technical assistance, help in building infrastructure, education and training in management and accounting, and trade access to all markets. They were disappointed with the lack of market access, and rightly or wrongly, they regard the West in this respect as hypocritical: It provides assistance for various things, but at the same time, keeps its markets closed to Eastern Europe. This lack of market access is particularly true of the European Community. The Poles are in a position to export steel, textiles, and agricultural products, but none of those things are welcome in the European Community.

Briefly, my committee, the American Committee for Aid to Poland, was founded in the fall of 1989 as the result of work by David Gergen and John Richardson. John Richardson was an assistant secretary of state for education and cultural affairs for many years, and then president of Youth for Understanding. He also was president of Radio Free Europe. David Gergen, whose name you all know, served in the White House during the first Reagan administration and is a prominent journalist and political commentator.

David Gergen and John Richardson established this organization, originally called the Emergency Committee for Aid to Poland, to help Poland succeed in this transitional period. The co-chairmen of our supporting committee are Senator Bob Dole and Zbigniew Brzezinski. We are bipartisan, multiethnic, and try to help in various ways.

I chair a loose, unnamed consortium of private, voluntary organizations active in Poland. Our aim is to make U.S. assistance more effective. Additionally, our committee has its own programs in Poland, and we mainly focus on strengthening the "self-help sector," the private, generally voluntary, social-service sector. Currently, a great deal of activity is taking place in that area, with new organizations springing up all of the time. They do things that the government is not able to do and probably should not attempt.

I am convinced that self-help activities and community development are basic elements in building democracy. In our activities, not only do we help individuals in need, but we help people to help themselves and to build associations and communities in which they are better able to manage their own affairs.

MR. WIRT: I am honored to be here, and especially to be able to participate with Mr. Malone, whom I deeply respect. I learned of Mr. Malone and the American Committee through a book by A.E. Dick Howard called *Democracy's Dawn*.

I am going to cover two areas: first, the effort of Virginia managers to help Polish managers, and second, some challenges and problems, as I see them, for Polish local governments. By Virginia managers, I mean the county, city, and town managers in Virginia and their professional association (the Virginia Local Government Management Association) which I staff.

Last May, the International City/County Managers' Association invited me to be their representative at a United Nations working group that focused on management problems in some of the world's megacities, particularly in developing countries. Roman Dziekonski, the deputy mayor of Warsaw, Poland, was part of that group. During the course of the week we became friends, and he asked me to rally some of our local government managers to help with basic management skills in Poland. I readily agreed. As a starting point I have made two trips to Poland and spent about 15 days there, traveling throughout the country and meeting with Polish administrators from nine different cities. Our managers' association has linked 40 current or retired Virginia managers with 16 Polish managers in a program we term "Managers to Managers."

The term *manager* is not commonly used, at least not yet, in the Polish local government setting. Polish city councils are large, typically with 50 elected members. They appoint a president who is sometimes called the mayor, but in our terminology, he is the manager. The president works full-time, administrating in the local government. He or she is usually joined by one or two deputies that the president recommends and the council approves. The council appoints a couple of other people to work with them. These five to seven people become the governing body of the locality.

9

Essentially, they are the administrative arm. The lead person, however, is the mayor of the local government, whom I call the manager.

The Virginia Local Government Management Association was enthusiastic to see what could be done in Poland. Last fall we began by collecting a wide array of literature that our Virginia local governments use with our citizens. This literature was distributed throughout Poland. The deputy mayor of Warsaw along with some of his fellow managers had suggested the types of information they felt would be most useful. One example of literature sent is this town calendar of Blacksburg, Virginia. The calendar is actually the town's annual report to its citizens. On each month of the calendar, Blacksburg includes the dates the city council and the planning commission meet and a few civic functions, such as basketball games. As one goes through the calendar, information is provided on the town council, town manager, town attorney, fire department, police department, Chamber of Commerce, self-help telephone numbers, etc.

The managers in Poland do not need for us to tell them what to do or how to do it. They need ideas. This is their first experience with local democracy, so we are trying to provide ideas. We are trying to send only material that is very basic and practical. Ideally, our literature would all be in Polish, but we compromised and have translated the cover notes into Polish.

The head of a Polish school of business and administration told me that they suffer from a lack of literature. He said that they do not have time to wait for everything to be translated. Only one in three Polish managers may be sufficiently skilled in English to directly use our information. I found that in most communities, however, someone on the staff who is at a fairly high level can review the information. We do plan on translating some simple pamphlets into Polish, such as tips on good management and developing and implementing a local government budget. Also our retired Virginia managers have sent letters stating a few key challenges that they faced as local government managers and the management approach used to solve them.

We have invited the deputy mayor of Warsaw to come to the annual meeting of our professional association this spring. We also plan to bring someone to attend the Senior Executive Institute (SEI), a two-week training course for local government managers here at the University of Virginia. We are looking at our manager-to-manager program as a long-term effort, and hope to have a Polish manager attend SEI on an annual basis.

Finally, we are in the last stages of applying for a grant from the United States Information Agency that would fund approximately 20 internships between Polish and Virginia managers. Initially, we would send three recently retired Virginia managers to Poland for about six to eight weeks. The Virginia manager would work along side the Polish manager, observing and offering insights and alternatives based on many years of managing in a democratic setting. The Polish manager would later have the opportunity of interning with a Virginia manager here in the United States.

Our effort here in Virginia is certainly not the only effort to aid Polish local government. Many other key parties, such as the International City/County Managers Association, are also providing aid. We are trying to coordinate with all of the key players. As Mr. Malone told me when we first began, the need is so great that the threat of duplication is probably minimal. By coordinating, however, we can maximize our efforts.

I would now like to tell you my observations of some of the key challenges facing Polish local governments. The first three problems flow from Mr. Malone's presentation, so I will not spend much time on them. They are, however, a major factor in an efficient local government.

The first problem is the lack of a tradition of local self-government. No historical guideposts are available to follow in creating the system, which has led to a certain amount of foundering in approaching the problem.

The next problem relates to a growing number of citizens disillusioned with democracy. I was in Poland earlier this month and there is a growing feeling that democracy is not working. Many citizens feel lost, and their great expectations of moving quickly into the middle class are not being met. They think that maybe it will happen for their grandchildren, but not for them. These feelings hamper the enthusiasm to support and work with local governments.

The lack of grass-roots democracy—civic groups, self-help groups, volunteer activities, and their power within a community—is a problem. I grew up in a farming community where people made homemade ice cream. To get the temperature cold enough to freeze the ice cream, salt was added to the ice. Similarly, I view grass-roots democracy and these volunteer and civic groups as being the necessary ingredient to get the right mix for a democratic, working local government. As efforts of the American Committee and others continue to blossom, local governments will improve.

One of the big problems in Poland is the lack of good management skills, at least as people think of them in a democratic context. Most Polish local government managers are well educated. Many of them are engineers, which is an important quality, because they oversee a fair amount of infrastructure projects. But unlike American managers, they have not had the opportunity to attend schools of public administration for advanced degrees. They do not have the kind of professional associations that Americans have, where a manager attends annual training seminars and meets with fellow managers, although that type of association is beginning to develop. A number of people who would have been leading managers, however, left Poland in the 1980s. I read that half of Warsaw University of Technology's 1980 graduates left.

Fiscal stress is a major problem. We think we have fiscal stress here in our Virginia local governments, but consider this situation: In Poland, roughly 50 percent of local government revenues come from the national government, but three months into the local government's fiscal year, the national government has not set its budget. No monies have been distributed to local governments, and they do not know how much revenue they will receive. Likewise, local officials do not have a tradition of developing, administering, and auditing local budgets to ensure the most efficient use of the money that is available.

One issue in particular costs Polish local governments a great deal of money: communal housing. This housing in the form of high-rise flats was built extensively by the communist system throughout Poland. So it is more than just a minor problem. Rents are set so low that they do not come close to covering the cost of maintaining the property. The fact that the local government now owns the property instead of the national government does present real possibilities, because the local governments can privatize the property. Privatization creates problems, however, because the property has never been sold, and there is no way of determining its value. Also, even if some market value is set, affordable lines of credit are nonexistent, so people cannot easily obtain a mortgage and purchase the property. I am told that if the money were available, it is possible that the interest rates would be 40 or 60 percent a year, which is totally unrealistic. Bus systems also cause a lot of problems, because as you know from U.S. systems, you never collect enough money to cover expenses.

One final challenge I have time to mention is the size of the councils. These councils are learning how to work together. With 50 people, a tremendous number of ideas are generated. One manager told me that a council meeting was like parliament, and they went on forever. There was so much diversity, it was hard to manage.

Another related concern, from our perspective, is that all of the members of the council are up for election at the same time, without staggered terms. In our local governments, institutional knowledge, training, and continuity is built into the system by having staggered terms and trying not to have a majority of the council elected at one time. One of the challenges is the real possibility for wholesale changes, not only in the council but in the key staff who run the local governments.

Although I have mentioned a number of key challenges for Polish local governments, I am upbeat on Poland for the long term. There is great strength in the Polish people. They generally are well educated and eager to learn. They have a long history of overcoming difficult situations. Also, I have found it easy to get to know and to work with them. They are most appreciative of efforts such as ours.

NARRATOR: We have with us today a Fulbright scholar from Poland who perhaps has some comments or questions.

POLISH SCHOLAR: I deeply appreciate your kind attitude toward my country and your understanding of our basic problems. I agree with all of your statements.

I would like to make the following remarks concerning the future of the Polish political system. There are three scenarios. The best scenario is the democracy-participation scenario in which a democratic Poland will join the global market economy. This scenario is the best one, and I am convinced that in the long term, we will be successful in achieving this desired state.

The second scenario is the pink scenario, which is connected with former Communists. They now call themselves Social Democrats. They present more or less rational programs, step-by-step, throughout the free-market economy. They are Populists, and want to provide Poland with a social security system, schooling system, and medical system. They can be successful to a certain extent. They will never have any power in Poland by themselves, however, but only as part of a coalition.

I personally consider the worst scenario to be the ultra-nationalist scenario with aggressive nationalism attempting to create another primitive identity. A few growing nationalist parties are growing in Poland. They consider Poland a unitary nation. Who is a true Pole? Who is an untrue Pole? Are only Catholics true Poles? Who is to blame for the present situation?

They think we can find a fair way between socialism and capitalism, which is, of course, not true. They say, "Give us power. We will make you rich next year." The people who are unemployed, who have no access to a good medical system or good schools, will follow them. I hope in the long term that our destiny will be to join all of Europe.

I really appreciate your understanding of the existence of Polish local government. From my sociological perspective, I think that the Communists cancerously destroyed local towns and communities, because local governments were considered to be a kind of underground rebellion against Communist power. What is abroad today is a post-Communist consciousness. I would say, however, that a homo-Sovieticus still lives in Poland, a Sovietized person who is now living in a system of freedom. He still behaves and thinks like he is living under a Communist system. The Sovietized person

14

is against local governments. He withdraws, and looks for recommendations and directions. He likes to follow, which is what has been taught for 40 years. He has been taught not to be independent in thinking and in action.

Negativism is also present. Some have a habit of denying and rejecting. For 40 years, they have had a negative strategy to reject the Communist social lifestyle. Now they are expected to make an important, conscious shift from passivism to activism, from negativism to constructivism. How to make this shift with these same people is like a big puzzle. We must reshape this puzzle, and we need time.

I fully support your long-term optimism. What does long term mean: one decade or one hundred years? I am hoping that we will be successful in less than a century.

MR. MALONE: I agree with what you have said. I certainly hope that your first scenario is the one that works. I think you are right in saying that the Communists have left a legacy in which people look to the central authority to solve their problems.

At the conference I attended last June, I was assigned to a working group headed by a Polish senator whom I know, Doctor Kuratowska. She had been talking to constituents, and in small localities people would come to her and complain about something that was happening in their particular village. They looked to the senator from Warsaw to solve their particular local problems. I think that attitude often arises. It's a natural legacy, but certainly it is important to encourage people to change.

POLISH SCHOLAR: It is difficult for me to change myself in two or three years. I have been taught to look for recommendations and directions, and not to be free. We understand now that freedom is not just a gift; democracy is not just a gift, it is an experience. It is a historical experience we must go through.

MR. MALONE: The American Committee for Aid to Poland is supporting something called the Ochota Association of Self-Help Groups. Ochota is a district of Warsaw in the way Queens is a part of New York City. Its members are groups that formed in the last two or three years and, with some encouragement from ACAP, formed the Ochota association and elected a chairman. We are trying to help this association, and the motivation is precisely of the sort to which you have referred. These people want to do things for themselves and solve their own problems. They have no experience yet in doing that, but it is a sign, I think, that a lot of things are possible. We have supported the creation of a data base of such groups throughout Poland, and over a thousand organizations have been identified. So, this is an example of the positive side.

QUESTION: How would the Polish government go about trying to privatize these big state industries? They could incorporate them and sell stock, but who is going to buy them, and where do they get the money? Also, who is going to organize the corporate management structure? Isn't that a major problem of starting from zero and building to a private enterprise structure?

MR. MALONE: It is a huge problem, and the fact is, the government has not yet decided how to do it, which is also a big problem. Many schemes have been suggested. Plans have been adopted, and at various stages, they have presented ways to solve the problem, but they have not worked.

A plan was proposed to hire a number of Western experts to set up nationwide mutual funds through which people could hold shares in these companies, but it was never implemented. Some enterprises could be sold to foreigners, but that proposal creates two problems: One, not everyone wants the best parts of the state sector to be owned by foreigners, especially Germans. Second, there are not many plants that foreigners would want to buy, because most are unprofitable. Determining profitability is difficult, because profitability never played a role in the old economic system. They are still struggling with this problem of valuation.

The Czechs have recently embarked on a different scheme in which shares are either sold for a small amount or given out to the public, and the public becomes shareholders. The plan is enormously difficult and relatively little progress has been made. Then, the social cost must be considered. Many of the state-owned factories in Poland are grossly overstaffed and terribly inefficient. The state sector has already begun laying off people. There is not an easy answer to privatization, and that is why some people are beginning to talk about slowing down the process. Whether that is good or bad, I am not sure.

QUESTION: Some weeks ago we had here some members of the Polish parliament who were touring the United States. One made a statement that although Russian troops had been withdrawn from Hungary and Czechoslovakia, they still remain in Poland. Is the army a large threat that the Poles worry about?

MR. MALONE: I do not think it is regarded as a threat, but it certainly is a sore point. The negotiations for troop withdrawal have continued since approximately 1990. The Soviets argued initially that those troops were needed to protect the supply lines to the Soviet forces in East Germany. Since they lost East Germany, the Soviets have said, "We really need those troops there until all of our boys come home from Germany."

The commanding general of the Soviet forces in Poland is very arrogant. Initially, he barely deigned to talk, but from what I read, the negotiations continue. I'm sure they will eventually be removed.

QUESTION: You mentioned 29 parties. Is that a threat to democracy? How much is proportional representation and the multiparty legislature likely to stall things and make the third scenario more likely? Is there any chance of setting up a two-party system the way it is in this country and the United Kingdom?

MR. MALONE: I would say there probably is not any chance of setting up a two-party system, but many people are concerned that as many as 29 parties are now in parliament. An even greater number of parties exist in Poland that were not elected.

Some commissions in parliament are thinking about these issues: What kind of representation is needed? Is it really sensible to have such a large number? It all happened so fast that it is expecting too much for the people to suddenly develop a perfect governing scheme. They are still thinking about it.

17

Another problem in Poland is that they have to solve so many problems at once. You can imagine what it is like to be a representative in the Polish parliament. All of the laws have to be changed. A new structure has to be created. The constitution has to be rewritten. They are trying to accomplish all of these things simultaneously, and it is an enormous job. Many people are thinking about the future and wondering whether this system is exactly right.

QUESTION: Polish farmers resisted collectivization and exercised a certain amount of independence. Does this attitude manifest itself now in their activity? Is there anything more encouraging on the agricultural side than in the cities?

MR. MALONE: An ironic situation now in Poland is private farming. The Communists never succeeded in collectivizing more than a portion of it, and most remained as private, small farms. These people were independent and one of the bulwarks against central authority. You would suppose, therefore, that they would be delighted with the new economic system, but they are not because they received subsidies and fixed prices under the old system. A considerable movement has arisen, which I do not pretend to fully understand, among the agricultural parties for an increase in subsidies. It may be a lack of understanding.

I have already quoted Professor Geremek, but I will do so once more. In our conversation in January, he told me, "One of our current political problems is to get the peasant parties to form a coalition with us, and to do that, we have to convince them that centralized direction of the economy is not in the long-term interest of the farmers, but they do not understand that." So, it is a curious situation.

QUESTION: I would like to ask a question of both speakers. First to Mr. Wirt, you mentioned the two-week executive leadership seminar here. One of the techniques most effectively employed there might be useful in Poland, and I wondered if you have been able to transfer it—namely, using discussion groups to talk about mutual problems and different solutions. There is a sense that locally people can create their own answers. The question for Mr. Malone is to tell us how we can get through an hour of discussion of Poland and never mention Lech Walesa or the Catholic church. What about those institutions?

MR. WIRT: A discussion group is an excellent idea that we can try when our retired managers go to Poland. We have not yet had the opportunity to use this approach. Discussion groups can help instill confidence that as individuals and local officials we have the power to bring about change and help solve our own problems. We do not need to wait on others to tell us the solutions. Your suggestion for using discussion groups is a good one.

MR. MALONE: How this discussion could last for an hour without the Catholic church being discussed is a good question. The attitudes towards the church in Poland are changing. The church played an enormously important role under the Communist regime as a symbol of anti-Communism and Polish patriotism. You cannot exaggerate the importance of the church in that period. I remember when I lived there, seeing the churches on Sunday with people spilling out into the street because there was not enough room in them. The battle with communism has been won, however, and I think you could say that the church is now turning to more traditional concerns about the work of the church itself and social questions. At the same time, at least a certain proportion of people who previously went to mass and supported the church for patriotic reasons no longer do so. For example, the abortion issue is currently a tremendously heated debate in Poland, more so than in the United States. It is a bitter discussion. This debate involves the issues of education and divorce. I find that people do not talk much about the church. If I raise the question, they will talk about it, but it is not something that is uppermost in people's minds.

As for Lech Walesa, part of the problem is that the president does not have much of a role in Poland. The presidency was first held by General Jaruzelski, when it was just as well that the president did not have much of a role. After the 1989 elections parliament was only partially Communist, and Jaruzelski began to play—and this statement is probably an oversimplification—an essentially ceremonial role.

Walesa made a lot of promises. He talked about how he was going to wield the ax and get things done, and he was elected. The question is, however, how will things get done? He discovered, as people do in many countries, that things were really more complicated than he assumed when he was running for office. Second, there was not any way to get things done. At first, a great deal of talk was heard after he was elected about trying to persuade the parliament to allow him to rule by decree, which they were not about to do. That issue still comes up from time to time.

The question is, what kind of role can he play? I think he can be a public leader and educator. Although Walesa sometimes says things he does not really mean, he is a natural politician and has a real feel for what people are thinking. But he has not always known what to say. He has, as far as I can determine, basically supported the economic reform process as it was designed. From time to time he speaks out about it.

He is doing some useful things abroad too, despite having complained in a recent speech about foreigners investing in Poland. He was recently in Germany and asked the Germans to invest more money. He is thinking about larger issues too. Again, when I go to Poland, no one is talking about Walesa. If they are talking politics, they are talking about what is happening in parliament.

QUESTION: On the question of Russian troops in Poland, some are still left in Germany, and Germans are helping with economic aid for them in Russia. Couldn't Western aid be used to help the withdrawal of the Russian army from Poland?

MR. MALONE: I think the problem is not so much the large number of Soviet troops in Germany, but that they do not have a place to go when they get back. Therefore, as you say, the German government is giving economic aid. Although the Soviets have behaved badly on this issue, they do believe that the troops in Poland are part of their line of communications, and once the troops are out of Germany, they will leave Poland. I do not think Western economic incentives would change the situation much. In terms of numbers, the number of troops in Poland is not huge. It does not compare with the number still in Germany. Some of them are leaving, but it is happening gradually.

COMMENT: Not incentives, but the United States or the IMF could withhold money until they leave.

MR. MALONE: Yes, I suppose it could, but the United States is involved in a much larger game in the Soviet Union, and whether that would damage its other goals in the Soviet Union, I do not know. I would be inclined to keep prodding them, but probably not threaten them financially at this point.

NARRATOR: Dumas Malone, who always asked the last question, is not here today, but if he were, or if his spirit is somewhere around us, I'm sure he would be proud of his son, the first speaker. He also would be very pleased that we have discovered a second speaker who is equally committed to this area, and in that vein, we thank both of you.

II.

CONSTITUTIONAL AND POLITICAL CHANGE IN POLAND

CHAPTER TWO

The Polish Political Scene, the Walesa Presidency, and the Parliamentary Elections*

LESZEK GARLICKI

NARRATOR: Professor Leszek Garlicki is no stranger to the Miller Center. He participated in a colloquium on constitutionalism of the United States, Poland, and France more than two years ago. He also has lectured here on the presidency, and in a sense, his lecture today is about the Polish presidency two years later, looking at the developments that have occurred since that previous lecture.

Professor Garlicki is a member of the Faculty of Law at the University of Warsaw. He has taught at a number of universities in the United States, including the Saint Louis University, the University of Indiana, the Law and Graduate Center at Capital University in Ohio, and the University of California.

He has written numerous works, including one on the United States Supreme Court. He has been especially interested in the interrelationship between Polish law and the Polish constitutions and other countries' law and constitutions. He was an adviser to a subsection of the Roundtable that planned and initiated the transition to democratic government in Poland. It is a great pleasure and honor to have him with us again, and once again we should thank Lady Blanka Rosenstiel for making this presentation possible.

Presented in a Forum at the Miller Center of Public Affairs on 22 May 1992.

MR. GARLICKI: I have had several opportunities to return to the Miller Center, and I am always glad and grateful to be able to do so. Two years ago I had the pleasure of presenting a lecture on the Polish Presidency. The situation was unclear then in Poland. In the summer of 1990, General Jaruzelski was still president of Poland, and two key functions, the Ministry of Defense and the Ministry of Police, were held by political friends of Jaruzelski who were former high-ranking members of the Polish Communist Party. Even if it were already well known two years ago that the Communist system had more or less ended, there was still the big, open question, what next? How would the transition toward some fully democratic system be conducted in Poland? What would be the price? What would be the timing?

Two years later, we can say that the Polish system of govern-ment is a legitimate one. It may not be fully democratic; it still may not be as developed as we would like it to be. Nevertheless, it is a legitimate system in the sense that the president was elected by popular vote in the fall of 1990, and the parliament was elected by a fully democratic electoral vote in October 1991. The question is, what next, and to what extent can the constitutional and democratic legitimacy of the system be translated into the system's ability to function effectively?

I am glad we do not have enough time here to discuss all of the problems because I am not compelled to discuss economic problems, which, as usual in Poland, are more confusing than political or democratic problems. Nevertheless, I will begin with some historical remarks.

Several historical similarities and examples could certainly be pursued today. The office of the president has a considerable tradition in Polish history. The presidency was first introduced in Poland in the so-called March Constitution of 1921. The presidency was maintained and expanded by the next constitution, the so-called April Constitution of 1935. So, the presidency had existed for a relatively long time between the two wars. It therefore has some tradition, but it is a strange tradition. The development of the Polish presidency before World War II was centered around one powerful political personality: Józef Piłsudski. Piłsudski was unquestionably the number-one politician in prewar Poland. He

26

was identified with the rebirth of Poland in 1918. He was also identified with the first three years of leadership of independent Poland, especially the successful war against Soviet Russia. Piłsudski was highly regarded as the national hero of Poland.

While he was highly regarded by the population, however, other politicians feared him. It was clear to them that they were no match for Piłsudski. If he were granted enough constitutional powers to combine his political position with his constitutional position, he would be a dictator of Poland, and the other politicians did not want a dictatorship. Consequently, the 1921 Constitution was written against Józef Piłsudski. The 1921 Constitution adopted a weak presidency based mainly on the French constitutionalism of the Third Republic. This weakness in the presidency created a process of government centered around the parliament and the cabinet.

It was clear that this constitution was written against Piłsudski, as a strong president and politician. If Piłsudski had wanted to be president, he would have been elected without any problem. But since, the constitution was made against him, it is not surprising that Piłsudski refused to be president. He retired and watched the political scene in Warsaw.

The political scene in Warsaw after 1921 was not encouraging. Parliaments were fragmented, and the numerous political parties were completely unable to reach compromises within the parliament. Within five years, there were a dozen cabinets. Generally speaking, even if the economic situation was not bad, the prestige of parliament and the political parties was diminishing.

Piłsudski watched the situation from some distance. It was clear that Piłsudski was still the supreme authority of the Polish military and that he had enough power to control the Polish army, regardless of the institutional arrangements. The situation resulted in a successful coup d'etat in May 1926. Following the coup, Poland entered a period of so-called *Sanacja* (a term used to describe Piłsudski's followers after 1926), when Józef Piłsudski alone ruled from 1926 until 1935.

Under the 1921 Constitution (which was maintained after the coup), Piłsudski still did not want to be the president. Ignacy Mościcki was appointed president of Poland, but it was obvious that it was Piłsudski—sometimes as prime minister, sometimes as minister of the army, sometimes as general inspector of the army—who led Polish politics. At the same time, Piłsudski tried to get a new constitution for Poland. It was another irony in Polish history that only a month after the new constitution was finally adopted in April 1935, Piłsudski died of cancer. It was then impossible to give a strong presidency with enormous powers to another person to exercise those powers as Piłsudski would have done. As a result, the 1935 Constitution and the continuation of the Mościcki presidency were not successful.

The next development was the 1952 Constitution adopted under the new Yalta system after World War II. Under this system, the real power belonged not to the state machinery, but to the Communist Party. As a matter of fact, the real power belonged not to Polish institutions—the Communist Party or any other institution—but to the Soviet Union. As the real mechanism of power was located in other places, the new "collective" presidency (the so-called Council of State) was only a nice decoration.

This same system was maintained throughout the next 38 years. The real power was concentrated within the central bureaucracy of the Communist Party. The real leader in Poland was the first secretary of the Communist Party, even if he did not hold any leading state position. Usually he was just a member of the Council of State.

In April 1989 a constitutional amendment, the so-called April Amendment, introduced many changes to the 1952 Constitution. Maybe the most important amendment introduced then was the reestablishment of the presidency. The question is, why? What happened in 1989 to make the institution of presidency again become so important and relevant for Polish politics? Once more, it was not the quest for democracy or an attempt to establish a better system. For purely political reasons, the presidency was introduced as one of the compromises adopted by the Roundtable. Roundtable talks between the Solidarity trade union and the Communist Party finally led to a compromise where three elements were most important. The first was that Solidarity was legalized and even invited to the parliament, but only as an opposition group. Second, the new parliamentary elections were set up to give a safe majority to the Communist Party and political friends of the Communist Party, the Peasant Party and Democratic Party. Third, the new presidency had a lot of power over parliament.

The idea then was that parliament, even with a Communist Party majority, was not as politically safe as it had been before. "So let's have another institution," said the leaders of the Communist Party. "Let's have a president." It was obvious that the presidency was a concession from Solidarity to the Communist Party. "Well, it's yours. You may have the presidency, and you may have the president." It was clear that the president would be Jaruzelski. As president, he was to ensure that the democracy, as it was called then, the semi-democracy, did not go too far.

The presidency, according to the April Amendment, has become a powerful position. The president was then elected by parliament. He could be dismissed only by a complicated impeachment procedure, and he had a great deal of legislative power, including the veto. The president had exclusive power to nominate the prime minister, but no power to dismiss the cabinet. Once the cabinet was in office, the president practically had no power to control it. Only parliament could dismiss the cabinet. Once the cabinet has been dismissed, however, it was once more the president, and only the president, who could propose a nominee to be the new prime minister to parliament. The president had the power to dissolve parliament, but only in three situations. One is when the parliament is unable to form a government, a cabinet, within three months. The second is when the parliament is unable to adopt a state budget within three months. The third is when parliament adopts legislation that endangers the constitutional position and functions of the president. No one knew what that meant, but it gave greater discretionary freedom to the president.

The president was the commander in chief of the Polish army and also ex-officio chairman of the National Council of Defense. The constitution divided the responsibility for the military between the president as the commander in chief and the minister of defense, who was subordinate to the prime minister and parliament. Clearly, there were two different avenues for controlling the army.

Those powers, or generally speaking, those regulations concerning the presidency were written in unclear language and left room for interpretation. This lack of clarity was purposely included to make it possible for General Jaruzelski to exercise almost any version of the presidency.

In April 1989, no one was even dreaming about the Solidarity government in Poland. No one even imagined that something like a general fall of communism in Eastern Europe or the Soviet Union could ever happen. Given the scenario, it was a careful compromise, making it possible for Solidarity to exist again, but at the same time, giving the Communist Party and its president very strong powers to control events within this new democracy or semi-democracy.

It was not astonishing that General Jaruzelski was elected president by the Polish parliament, even if it was astonishing that he was elected by only a one-vote majority. Shortly after Jaruzelski was elected president, however, he encountered a completely new political situation, a complete change in political climate. The majority held by the Communist Party in parliament disappeared quite rapidly. Two small parties that had always been associated with the Communist Party changed sides in favor of Solidarity. Suddenly it was possible for Solidarity to have a majority in parliament. The most important problem, though, was in the international context when other East European countries quickly began to change their systems.

Consequently, Jaruzelski never tried to implement his impressive powers. His presidency was timid and careful. The real process of government was conducted by Tadeusz Mazowiecki as the prime minister and, of course, Lech Walesa. Walesa was not even a member of parliament. He was just Mr. Walesa, a person who create Solidarity and eliminate the Communist Party from Polish politics even though he did not have a formal position.

In 1990 it was clear that Poland needed to have the president popularly elected. At the same time, however, two important political developments paralleled each other. One was the elimination or the disappearance of the Communist Party. Even if technically the party still had more than 100 members in parliament, the Communist Party as such ceased to exist, and it was relatively certain that its members would not act together.

The second, more important development was the split within Solidarity. The number of parliamentary seats controlled by the Communist Party did not change much from June 1989 to October 1990. In September 1989 the Communist Party had 173 deputies and the Solidarity Caucus (OKP) had 161 deputies. In September 1990 the Democratic Left (post-Communist) Caucus had 104 deputies. But at the same time, instead of the one civic Solidarity caucus there were several new organizations, illustrating the apparently irreversible Solidarity split. Thus, this fragmentation of Solidarity finally determined the presidential elections in the fall of 1990 in which there were six candidates.

The constitution had been changed, and now the president was to be elected, not by parliament, but by popular vote. It was not astonishing that both Walesa and Mazowiecki wanted to be president. Other politicians participated in the elections as well. What was astonishing, however, was that Walesa did not get the necessary 50 percent to be elected in the first round. Perhaps even more astonishing, it was not Mazowiecki who finished second, but the relatively unknown businessman, Stanislaw Tymiński, the leader of party X. The second round of the presidential election was a duel between Walesa and Tymiński, ending in an easy victory for Walesa, who received 74.3 percent of the vote.

Nevertheless, the presidential elections produced one important, but dangerous, result for Polish politics. Walesa and Mazowiecki understood that they did not have as clear and strong a support of the Polish electorate as they had presumed. This understanding determined their position toward the coming parliamentary election.

The first trial for the new president was to make the old parliament dissolve itself after adopting a new, democratic electoral law. The biggest question in Poland in the spring of 1991 was what kind of electoral law should be adopted. One choice was an electoral law based on proportional representation for all existing parties and organizations. Under proportional representation, 15 percent of the votes would mean 15 percent of the seats. The alternative was some system of majoritarian representation, under which stronger parties would win more seats than their percentage of votes and weaker parties would be eliminated.

In the spring of 1991, Walesa, counting on his popularity, seemed to prefer a majoritarian system. At the same time, Mazowiecki's Democratic Union and the Communist Party feared any kind of majoritarian system. They calculated that they could lose the election and fail badly under any type of majoritarian system. As a result, the majority of parliament began to advocate a purely proportional system.

Eventually even Walesa was not sure if the majoritarian system was good for him. The problem was that Walesa, even as president, had failed to organize his own strong presidential political party. Finally, a compromise was sponsored by Mazowiecki's Democratic Union and accepted enthusiastically by the Communists. Remember that the Communists had more than 100 votes in parliament. It was a compromise for a pure or almost pure proportional system that would give democratic and fair representation in parliament. As a result, after the election, 29 different parties were represented in parliament. The most difficult problem is that no single party has more than 15 percent of the seats.

The two strongest parties, Mazowiecki's Democratic Union and the Communist Party, both have about 60 seats in parliament. It was very difficult to say even then exactly which party was Walesa's party and where the president stood within the parliament.

This fragmented parliament has caused many problems. Politically, on the Right is the Confederation for an Independent Poland (KPN) Party. Next is the Seven, also called the Small Coalition—a combination of peasant parties, Christian democratic parties, and Walesa's former party, the Center Alliance. To their left is the Three—the Democratic Union, Liberal Democratic Congress, and Polish Economic Program—which is a center-left coalition centered around Mazowiecki's Democratic Union. Finally, on the Left is the Democratic Left Alliance, the successor to the Communist Party.

Therefore, Walesa had to convince parliament to build a convincing majority out of this complicated mix of parties. Parliament's first attempt was the concept of the Five, a Right-Center coalition comprised of the KPN, Christian Democratic parties, and others. It did not work. Finally, the Small Coalition—the Seven—was able to create the government cabinet with Jan Olszewski as prime minister. At the same time, the coalition of the Three as well as the KPN and the Social Democratic Party formed the opposition. The Three might be willing one day to enter into the Seven. If so, a big coalition of ten political parties would result, but that is a question for the future. Thus, it was clearly a success for Walesa to have the ability to make parliament appoint a cabinet. At the same time, however, it was a failure for Walesa in that the cabinet was fragmented and losing support within parliament.

I would like to give you two examples of how difficult the life of the president, even with such strong powers, is today. The first example is the budget. Briefly, there is a controversy over whether the budget should follow some austerity economic program, or be much more generous toward spending for social benefits. An austerity program would probably be the healthiest thing for the Polish economy, but it would not receive widespread acceptance by Polish voters. Therefore, politically it is tempting to provide more money for social benefits and other spending. Economically, it is very difficult; it is almost impossible.

The effect is that as of May, there is still no budget. This budget should have been accepted by parliament several months ago. Still, the president has been careful not to intervene in the budget procedures, even though after three months he has the power to dissolve the parliament. Walesa now has an opportunity, at least, to dissolve parliament if he wishes to do so.

The other example is much more specific—the Polish army. There were three different actions last month concerning the army. The first involved a decision of the new minister of defense, under the new cabinet, to remove the former minister, who is a Polish admiral, by sending him into retirement. This decision was made against the will of Walesa, who had wanted to have the admiral appointed to an important position within the army. It was clear that the cabinet wanted to take control of the army.

The next action occurred when Walesa went to Germany for a state visit. Suddenly both the minister of defense and the minister of police dismissed their respective chiefs of intelligence, who were rather important people. This decision was made without any consultation with the president. Thus, an important question immediately arose about the position of the president as commander in chief of the armed forces. Should he have had some right to say yes or no?

The third action was the minister of defense's declaration before the press that certain politicians had acted to involve Polish army officials in "political games." The minister's remarks were interpreted as allusions to plots for a coup d'état. As a result, the president and the parliament asked for an investigation, and the minister of defense was sent on a holiday by the prime minister. Nevertheless, it is an illustration of how even sensitive problems, such as the Polish army, are now the object of a power play between the president, the cabinet, and parliament.

Is there some kind of historical analogy today to the situation that existed in the mid-1920s? Yes and no. Yes, in the sense that clearly the prestige and authority of parliament is shrinking. The prestige and authority of most political parties are also diminishing. While the authority of the president is also weak, at least there is some kind of charisma or understanding that the president is Lech Walesa and that he still has enormous possibility and power to act.

What is the difference? The most important difference is that Walesa was unable to build his own strong political party. Now, even if parliament were dissolved, the electoral law was changed, or attempts were made to establish a more reasonable political composition of the government, it would be difficult for the president to say, "This is my party. Vote for me and vote for my party." This is probably the biggest failure of Walesa today.

What are the gains of the president? In my opinion, the biggest gain is that the system is working; it is acting upon some democratic pattern. The gossip concerning a coup d'état suggested some repetition of the May 1926 scenario. At least, it was unfounded.

QUESTION: What articles or amendments in the U.S. Constitution will Poland have difficulty implementing, and why?

MR. GARLICKI: I suppose most of them. As far as the machinery of government is concerned, the presidential system of the United States is very different from all versions of presidencies ever

34

adopted in Europe. Even those who advocate a strong presidency in Poland are trying to imitate the French Constitution of 1958, not the American Constitution, which is generally regarded as giving too many powers to the president. Maybe for the United States, this system can work after 200 years of democracy, but for young and inexperienced democracies, it is very dangerous.

The second problem is that the Constitution of the United States is a federal constitution. The problem of federalism does not exist in Poland. At least we have one less problem. As far as federalism is concerned, once more, there is no reason to imitate.

Finally, there is the U.S. Constitution's Bill of Rights. This document is the bill of rights of a democratic country, of a country that has never had any serious experience with totalitarian regimes. That is why the U.S. Bill of Rights could be elaborated in general terms and be left for the judicial branch to interpret. From the point of view of East European countries, it is not precise enough. For this reason, the German, Spanish, and Portuguese constitutions, created after an era of totalitarianism, are better for East European countries. Under these constitutions, everything is written down, and it is clear what is prohibited by the government.

Probably the only, but not unimportant, guidance from the American Constitution is in regard to the position of the judicial branch and the notion of judicial review. It has been adopted in Western Europe and should now be adopted in Eastern Europe. As far as other developments are concerned, this country is so completely different even from West European countries that to try and bring something mechanically to Eastern Europe would be complicated.

QUESTION: The United States has the separation of church and state, which is very strong. Poland is known as a strong Christian country. How does that element affect Poland, and does the church have any influence on politics in Poland?

MR. GARLICKI: As a matter of fact, the church deserves enormous credit for bringing about the Polish revolution. The church, of course, was one of the main architects behind the emergence of Solidarity, its survival under martial law, and its success in the late

1980s. Therefore, while it might be interesting from a constitutional point of view, it is politically impossible to introduce the American version of the First Amendment, the non-establishment clause, with a wall of separation between church and state. It is impossible to transmit an experience from the United States, which has always been a country of different, more or less equal denominations to a country where the Catholic church is the church of 85 or 90 percent of Poles and has enormous political power.

QUESTION: How can so many political parties maintain memberships, raise funds, and formulate positions between elections?

MR. GARLICKI: I honestly do not know the answer to that question. Most of the political parties appeared shortly before the October 1991 elections. How many of them will be able to survive until the next elections is still an open question. Perhaps six or seven parties are already strong and established: the Democratic Union of Mr. Mazowiecki; the Confederation for an Independent Poland, the right-wing party of Mr. Moczulski; the Christian National Union of Mr. Chrzanowski and his group; maybe the Center Alliance—but only because it used to be Walesa's party and now is trying to survive without and even against Walesa; and the former Communist Party—the Democratic Left Alliance—which is not a very big party, but is maybe the best organized. Those five plus one of the peasant parties constitute a kind of backbone for the Polish system. They think of different ways to acquire membership and money. These parties have already existed for two years, which in post-Communist Eastern Europe is a long time.

QUESTION: Is the Polish Diaspora having any influence on modern Poland?

MR. GARLICKI: Probably not in a political sense. It has a great deal of influence on economic problems and the development among foreign governments of favorable attitudes toward Poland. The Polish Diaspora is trying to do its best, especially in encouraging foreign investment in Poland. This encouragement is not always supported by the present Polish government, but that is another problem.

QUESTION: What is the status of the Soviet army? Mazowiecki presumably asked them to stay to ensure the borders of Poland, but now that seems to be an academic problem.

MR. GARLICKI: The main reason was political. Mazowiecki did not want to alienate and disappoint Mikhail Gorbachev with an unnecessary demonstration during the talks about German reunification—this move was essential. Second, it was a money problem. "Let's make the Soviet army leave, but also, let's make the Soviet army pay for it." In 1990 that was not so unreasonable.

Today, the situation is different, and it is not clear who will fund the troop withdrawal. The main concern of the present Polish cabinet is that the Soviet army leave as soon as possible, but the political importance of the Soviet army in Poland is negligible.

QUESTION: I am a bit puzzled about the relationship between the prime minister and the president. It seems that once appointed, the prime minister only has responsibility to parliament and no responsibility to the president.

MR. GARLICKI: That assumption is correct. It is the traditional parliamentary system of Europe. Once the cabinet is appointed by parliament, it is responsible to parliament. Only parliament can dismiss a minister with a vote of censure. The president only has the exclusive power to propose prime minister nominations to parliament and approve the prime minister's nominations for cabinet positions. Walesa behaved loyally in his use of this power. He was not happy with the choice of Prime Minister Olszewski, and he made it clear that he wanted someone else. Nevertheless, once a majority in parliament accepted Olszewski, Walesa agreed to nominate him.

QUESTION: Doesn't that division of power result in a weaker president?

MR. GARLICKI: It is a clear limitation of the presidency, and in the United States, it would be against the very essence of the presidential system. Under French and British traditions, normally the head of state does not supervise the cabinet.

NARRATOR: What about Walesa's efforts to strengthen himself and limit parliament?

MR. GARLICKI: There is a proposal in parliament to change the constitution. The revisions, known as the Small Constitution, would intervene in state machinery, giving the president more power over cabinet nominations and dismissals and the legislative process. Under the current fragmented parliament, the legislative procedure is ineffective, and most of the adopted laws reflect a compromise among many parties. The president would like to have the power to make laws by decree. Parliament would have the power to reject the law, but not to amend it.

Ironically, during the 1989 Roundtable talks, Solidarity fought categorically against any type of presidential legislation, because it was regarded as dangerous. In 1981 the Council of State introduced martial law through extraparliamentary legislation. When Solidarity won in 1989, the president had no legislative power. Now Walesa has to deal with the consequences of his own proposals at the Roundtable.

QUESTION: Is it true that a few weeks ago, the heads of a Polish financial institution—similar to a U.S. savings and loan—absconded to Israel with $400 million?

MR. GARLICKI: It is an interesting case in terms of international law. The version given by these two fellows is that they are still able to control the finances of the institution, but they feel better in Israel because in Poland there was unjustified interference from the government. The other version, of course, is that they are crooks and should be put in jail.

Since both men are Jewish, they claimed Israeli citizenship when they arrived in Israel. Hence, extradition to Poland is possible under Israeli law. There is only one precedent that I know of in the history of Israel where a Jew was refused Israeli citizenship due to his criminal background, and he was returned to his former country. Whether the precedent will be followed in this situation is an open question.

NARRATOR: A question that Americans ask themselves is, will Poland make it? If Poland cannot make it, who can make it in Eastern Europe?

MR. GARLICKI: The problem is who will take over East European markets. The former Soviet republics may be less reliable politically, while Czechoslovakia, Hungary, and I hope Poland may be more reliable politically as well as economically. My feeling is that those markets are still available and could be won in the next five years without considerable cost by almost every economic power willing to invest. The question is, by whom? Germany will be the market leader unless other powers like Japan or the United States show some economic interest in Eastern Europe now.

The second question is whether those markets will be in democratic or totalitarian countries. My answer would be rather mixed. Probably some of the East European countries will be democratic; some will not make it. I hope Poland will make it.

It should be remembered that forms of really totalitarian regimes historically have been foreign to Poland. Even when nondemocratic regimes existed, those regimes were mild compared to some other countries and historical developments. Maybe with all of these quarrels and political fragmentations, we will be able to make it. I hope so.

LADY BLANKA ROSENSTIEL: I was in Poland in March, and I am very optimistic. I hear that many people are making it. They feel they are finally getting freedom, and they are trying. It is probably going to be the most difficult for the elderly who do not have much support in the new government. Otherwise, I think that young Polish people certainly want to seize the opportunity to become wealthy. They are struggling, but I am very optimistic about it. Don't you think so, Mr. Garlicki?

MR. GARLICKI: I hope so. There simply is no other alternative. Even the worst alternatives, like military rule and authoritarian regimes, have been tried by Jaruzelski. Everyone in Poland now understands that those types of regimes could not work, so maybe this is another reason to be optimistic.

To finish on an optimistic note, the cabinet recently said that first-quarter inflation was under 3 percent. For Poland, this report is important because it indicates that at least their austerity program, which is very austere, is functioning. It could be important.

NARRATOR: We thank Mr. Garlicki for this most informative presentation, and Lady Blanka Rosenstiel for making this presentation possible.

POSTSCRIPT

My lecture at the Miller Center was delivered two weeks too early. In the beginning of June 1992, the long pending controversies between President Walesa and the Olszewski Cabinet climaxed in a spectacular crisis.

In the end of May, the *Sejm* adopted a resolution directing the minister of interior to check whether those currently holding top state positions (from the president of the Republic to members of parliament, ministers, and judges) had collaborated with the secret police during the Communist era (this screening process is known as "the Lustration" process in Poland). Since no procedural regulations had been adopted, the whole action degenerated into a political conflict: Many influential names "leaked" to the public opinion and to the media without any possibility to verify whether the data were correct. On 4 June 1992 the *Sejm* adopted a motion of nonconfidence against the Olszewski cabinet (and on 19 June 1992 the Constitutional Court invalidated the *Sejm's* resolution as unconstitutional).

Upon the motion of President Walesa, the *Sejm* appointed Mr. Pawlak, the leader of the Polish Peasant Party, to the position of prime minister (at that time it was the *Sejm*, not the president that had an exclusive power to appoint and to dismiss the cabinet and/or its members). Pawlak was unable to form a majority cabinet, however, and finally, he resigned at the end of June.

At the same time, the Democratic Union and the Christian National Union entered successful coalition talks, and—with the concurrence of the president—they managed to build a new coalition of seven political parties. Mrs. Suchocka from the Democratic Union was appointed the prime minister, and after several days of bargaining, she was able to obtain the *Sejm's* approval for her cabinet.

Thus, the crisis ended in the creation of a new cabinet, with Mr. Olszewski and his allies landing on the opposition benches. It was a clear success for President Walesa as well as for the Democratic Union. Even if Suchocka's cabinet has been relying on a very shaky parliamentary majority, it was able to survive several confrontations (the conflict around the 1993 budget being the most spectacular one), and it is currently completing its ninth month of existence. Politically, as well as economically, there are more reasons now to be optimistic than was the case in May 1992.

Furthermore, the crisis of the summer of 1992 convinced political elites that the 1952 Constitution (as amended in 1989) had to be amended. The Constitutional Act of 17 October 1992 adopted an entirely new model of relations between the legislative and the executive branch. The amendment provided for two different versions of the government. As long as there is an absolute majority in the *Sejm*, it can control, dismiss, and appoint the cabinet, and the president has to comply with *Sejm's* decisions. If no absolute ("positive") majority can be built, the power shifts toward the president, who can appoint a "presidential cabinet" and—in some cases—dissolve the parliament. Taking into account the instability of the *Sejm's* political composition, President Walesa will intervene actively into Polish politics once the Suchocka's cabinet loses its parliamentary support.

Warsaw
6 April 1993

41

CHAPTER THREE

Political, Social, and Economic Developments and Dilemmas[*]

MACIEJ KOZLOWSKI

NARRATOR: It is a great pleasure to introduce Minister Counselor Kozlowski, the deputy chief of mission in the Polish Embassy in Washington. Few people can match the brave and successful efforts of Mr. Kozlowski.

He was a member of the editorial board of a Catholic newspaper, the *Universal Weekly*, in Kraków. For many years that paper was a platform for the opposition. After the withdrawal of martial law, the office of this newspaper provided a meeting place for members of the opposition and foreign statesmen, politicians, and journalists. In all of this, Mr. Kozlowski played a key role. He traveled around the world, spoke in a number of countries, and represented the opposition. In 1980 he became editor-in-chief of a Solidarity daily in Kraków. Before that, he had free-lanced and worked as a translator.

Mr. Kozlowski was sentenced to a five-year prison term in 1969 after a political trial, but was released after serving for two-and-half years. He had been charged with smuggling political literature into Poland.

He has been a lecturer at several universities in Poland, conducting, for instance, a university summer school for foreign students, and giving courses in a variety of fields and subjects. He has lectured in many American as well as European universities.

---

[*]*Presented in a Forum at the Miller Center of Public Affairs on 10 September 1992.*

Mr. Kozlowski has received several awards: the Nelly Strong Award for the best history book published in Poland in 1988; the Solidarity Award in 1986 for *Landscapes Before Battle*; and an award by the Polish Underground Union of Journalists for "preserving honesty in journalism." He has won other recognitions, and his stature and achievements are laudable. We are honored to have him with us.

MR. KOZLOWSKI: Thank you very much. Listening to that kind introduction seems like ancient history, in view of all of the changes in Poland. It seems so long ago that the Polish people had to fight for certain things. It is a lucky phenomenon, but it shows how things have changed in the last couple of years.

I am going to speak about the contemporary situation in Poland. I think Poland was and still is a country experiencing the most significant change that has taken place in 20th century history. It is a transition from communism to democracy, from a command economy to the market system. It means the historically unprecedented transformation of one-third of the world's population from one system to another in a very quick and profound, yet peaceful, way.

Some minor fights are occurring across the former communist landscape, but it is still a civilized transformation. It is important that Poland first demonstrated how this transformation could be done without bloodshed and violence. Poland is still leading the way in this transformation, serving as a kind of laboratory where events may be observed and later repeated in other countries.

Poland and Eastern Europe have lost the excitement they had three years ago with the Berlin Wall tumbling down, the mass demonstrations, and the euphoria of revolution. Now it is much more complicated, and therefore, there is not as much interest in Eastern Europe as there was three years ago. The events there, nevertheless, are very interesting.

To sum up the current situation in Poland, in the economic sphere, the most important arena, there is a bitter realization that this transformation is much more difficult, time-consuming, and costly than anyone expected two or three years ago. The worldwide expectation was that once communism was overthrown and the terrible waste came under better management, growth would be automatic and prosperity would come immediately.

The Polish people have learned that transformation from a command economy to a market economy is much more difficult and extremely costly. It is not a question of mismanagement or mistakes made in one country or another. The same problems are faced all over Eastern Europe, no matter who is in charge and which solutions are used.

The best example might be eastern Germany, where in spite of capital investment spending of DM 160 billion every year, or over $11,000 for each person, 30 or 40 percent of the people are still unemployed, and the economic situation is tense. The transformation has also created political tensions. The televised images of neo-Nazi violence in Germany show perfectly how the economic tension creates political tension and violence.

We in Poland do not have that kind of "rich uncle" as the east Germans have in the western part of their country. Poland does not have DM 160 billion poured into its economy every year. So we have had to struggle much more.

The same thing happened in Czechoslovakia and Hungary, although those two countries were in better shape when they started their reforms than Poland was. Reforms are also beginning in the former Soviet Union.

Our reforms began in January 1990, and were extremely successful. In one year's time Poland was able to establish a sound currency, which is now convertible. You can now buy whatever you wish without the use of coupons or another form of rationed distribution typical of the Communist era. Inflation, which had climbed to 2,000 percent in 1989, is now down to about 40 percent. It is still high, but it is not the hyperinflation that it used to be. Poland now provides a variety of goods and services, and looks like a normal Western country. The shops are fully stocked, with needed goods and services widely available.

This availability of goods and services has been the main change. The Polish people were raised in a situation where everything was scarce with demand always greater than supply. Life in that part of the world was always a fight for the few goods and services that were provided. Now the situation is different. Goods

45

and services are abundant, but the problem is that you need the money to buy them.

With these successes came a high price. First of all, this transformation started a very deep recession, which I need to put in perspective. A recession in the United States means that there is only about 1 percent growth yearly. Poland had about 12 to 25 percent decline in gross national product—a true recession.

The inevitable result of a recession is unemployment, which is now running at 13 percent, or approximately two million people. This is a very high number and especially painful, because unemployment was one of the things that the Communists claimed to have eradicated. They claimed they had full employment, and that in fact was how the system worked. It was a wasteful employment, of course, but at least people were employed. The state had to provide jobs, and no one had to worry about finding employment. Now the situation is different for many people, and it is a deep shock.

This unemployment figure of 13 percent must be qualified. Many of those unemployed would not work anyway, and are simply taking advantage of the system. Some unemployment was expected, but no one expected it to be quite so high when the reforms were introduced. A nice cushion was created in the form of high unemployment benefits. Sometimes people can earn more by claiming unemployment than by looking for a job. People are also eligible for benefits even if they have never worked. Accordingly, many housewives and many high school graduates claim unemployment; they get a "paid vacation," and they like it very much.

So, these safety nets created much of this unemployment. There certainly is unemployment, but as everyone will tell you, it is still very hard to find workers who are willing and able to do a job.

It is a question of geography. In big cities, it is still hard to find people to hire. It is a much more difficult situation in smaller towns, especially those where one factory previously had employed nearly all of the inhabitants of the town. This situation was the result of the typical Communist way of industrialization. They built a huge factory and a city around it, somewhere in an open field.

Now many of the factories, especially in the armament industry, are bankrupt and have had to fire people. The people in the small towns cannot find employment. With the shortage of housing, it is not easy to move from one place to another, and that creates problems. That is one of the reasons for the current wave of strikes. All of these problems have been on the economic level.

I think the transformation has been even more difficult at the psychological level. It was extremely tough for people. Even though everyone was fed up with communism, it is not easy to change one's way of life overnight. This change was especially difficult for people of a certain age who were accustomed to a given way of life and behavior. Now they have had to change completely. The younger people are coping better, while the older people are having trouble.

Employment is no longer automatic and housing is now a personal responsibility. Before, it was customary for the state to provide housing, but it was inadequate and difficult to get. People had to wait 20 years or, recently, even 50 years to get an apartment, but it was up to the government to provide housing. Health care was also free health care for everyone. Now the health-care system is in shambles because there is not enough money to provide for it. More and more services in the health system charge fees, something people find difficult.

I think the toughest aspect is that people now must earn money just to get the necessities of life. This is a hard change for many people who are used to a situation in which money was not that important. In the past a person would obtain special goods via connections or arrangements. There is an expression in Polish that means you do not buy things, you "arrange" things. Now people do not have to arrange anything; they simply go and buy it.

As an example, I received a letter from a friend who wrote that the situation is nice, but the old joy of life is over. Before, to get a nice piece of meat or cheese was an achievement of cunning and imagination. One had to hunt for it. Now this hunting spirit is gone, and as my friend wrote, the joy of life is over. He simply goes to a shop and buys whatever he wants.

Adapting to this new situation is not easy psychologically. Therefore, the psychological climate in Poland and in many other countries is kind of "blue." It is shocking for many people now traveling to Eastern Europe when they see all of the changes for the better, and still people are complaining and unhappy. This reaction is a very typical "blues" after the revolution, where the situation is changing and people have to adjust.

In such a psychological climate, it is natural that people are trying to find someone to blame for their troubles, especially those who are unemployed or fear unemployment and those who are left behind. Now the situation calls for totally new talents, new gifts from people. No longer is the working class considered the champion of progressive change.

The people who were once employed in big state factories constituted a sort of labor aristocracy, and they were the ones who created Solidarity. They overthrew the system, but now find themselves left behind. Their work is not needed anymore. The huge steel mills, armament factories, and the huge mines, which produce coal much more expensively than in other countries, are not needed anymore. These workers feel frustrated about this situation. They say, "We have overthrown the Communists, and now we are no longer needed." Their frustration has caused the wave of strikes that is now visible in Poland, and provides fertile ground for political extremists. I think Poland, once again, is leading the way in a difficult political phenomenon where radicalism is growing. When you feel that you are not well off and are insecure, you look for a scapegoat. It is easy to blame former Communists. Therefore, there is a radical, anti-Communist sentiment in a situation that is no longer communism.

To tell the truth, communism has never existed in Poland as a distinct entity. When I was lecturing in the United States, I was sometimes introduced as a person from Communist Poland. I always tried to explain that I was not from "Communist" Poland, because the only Communists I met in my life were on American campuses. I never met a Communist in Poland; I met a lot of them in America.

In Poland there were party members, but for the last 20 years, the Communist Party was something like an employment agency for managers. The Communists were not ideologues. They were a network of people supporting each other to get better jobs or a better piece of the pie.

They did ruin Poland to the very core, however, and it is true that they are responsible. The claim by many that there is a conspiracy of the former Communists still trying to govern Poland from behind the scenes, while now widespread in Poland, seems absurd to me. If they were so smart that they could run Poland clandestinely, they would never have lost power.

Those kinds of theories are abundant, and there is a growing sentiment for some kind of purge against former Communists. This sentiment motivated the government of Prime Minister Olszewski to disclose the files of the secret police. That prompted the dismissal of the government in June and a prolonged political crisis.

A difficult question that all of the former Communist countries are facing is what to do with the functionaries of the former regime. On one hand, the normal, human sense of justice demands that they be punished because they are, in many cases, criminals. They did some nasty things. As the press has quoted recently, it is unjust that a former secret police officer is receiving a 5 million zloty ($500) pension, two or three times the average salary. One of his victims, a person he arrested, is receiving only a 1 million zloty pension. It seems unjust.

On the other hand, trying to deal with the situation creates enormous problems. If these people to have to be brought to justice, how can it be done? Five "de-communization" projects are presently in parliament, but each of these projects ultimately leads to absurdity. For instance, there is a project to ban all former Communist apparatchiks from any managerial positions. That would seem to be fair. They were running the country for 45 years; they ruined it, so they should be excluded from running it now. If you look at the situation more closely, however, it's hard. If you decide to ban apparatchiks, you must first decide who is an apparatchik—which position, any party member? If membership in the party were the criterion, for instance, you would lose police, the army, and the fire department overnight, because everyone in these services had to be a party member. You cannot exclude these people because the country has to function.

Another criterion might be to rule out party functionaries, rather than every party member. But in what time period? If, for instance, you were a party functionary in the 1950s, and then you joined the opposition and fought for free Poland, should you be punished? Should people who never did anything to bring about the change be rewarded simply because they were never party members? That is another problem.

If you decide to purge party members, what about the other small parties that were even worse than the Communist Party? There were the fig-leaf "Democratic" and Peasant parties, which were supposed to represent a sign of pluralism in Poland, but were even worse than the Communist Party. If membership in any of these three parties is the criterion, you would have to purge about half of the population in Poland. Should these people be excluded from certain elected positions? The former Communists got a sound 10 percent of the vote in the free election. If you want to have a democracy, you cannot exclude someone because you do not like his views. These are the problems that are nagging Poland, as well as other countries. They will be extremely difficult to solve. This situation creates the tense political atmosphere that is so evident in Poland and other post-Communist countries.

I have given you a background, a general political outlook. As for recent developments, I am very happy, because for the last two months, all of the news coming from Poland has been good. The occurrence of this good news is rather strange, because there had been nothing but bad news. First of all, Poland was able to overcome the June crisis in a democratic way. A new government was formed in the beginning of July, and for the first time, it appears to have strong parliamentary support. The free election resulted in 29 parties in parliament, and no party had more than 12 percent support of the electorate. Because the parliament is extremely fragmented, creating a government is extremely difficult, and all of the previous governments were very weak. Now, the government of Mrs. Hanna Suchocka seems to have strong support in parliament and is the first government that is more or less coherent. It is made up of people who understand and work with each other. There is no infighting between the different government agencies.

Secondly, I think that personally, Mrs. Suchocka was a godsend for Poland. It is the first time that a woman has been head of the government. That is a good thing, because our political culture is not very high. Infighting in and out of parliament is sometimes nasty. Having a lady at the head of government—the Poles are rather respectful of ladies—creates a more gentle atmosphere in political quarrels. No one would go up to her and say anything nasty, because you do not say nasty things about ladies in Poland. She earned enormous respect from the population and is very popular, an important asset in politics. I think she has shown great resolve and strength, but in a mild manner that enabled her to deal with the strike situation.

At the time this government was created there was a wave of strikes, especially in the factories that were either going bankrupt or had been taken over by foreigners. These factories had some prospect for success, but the workers demanded the same wages that workers abroad get. It was absurd to demand the same level of wages in Poland as in the United States, because you would need the same level of productivity. Otherwise the factory would lose money.

For example, one of the Polish car factories was taken over by Fiat. The workers went on strike, demanding that their wages be 10 percent of the value of the cars they produced. Well, if they could produce the cars at the same speed as Detroit, maybe that would be just, but not at the speed of production in Poland. The strike is still continuing, unfortunately.

Other strikes occurred, but the government of Mrs. Suchocka proved to be tough. She said from the beginning that there would be no bargaining that would undermine the process of reform. The striking workers were demanding higher wages, which would have required changes in the system such as tax exemptions for factories. The government said no. If workers thought their factory was rich enough to pay higher wages, they could discuss it with the management. The government, however, would not interfere in a question between management and the workers. If the strikers' demands could be met without bankrupting the factory, that would be acceptable, but the reform program would not be changed. This was a tough position to take.

There was fear a month ago that this wave of strikes might spread and turn into a major crisis. Fortunately, it did not happen. Mrs. Suchocka and her government deserve a great deal of credit for their tough position and the fact that they were able to deal with a very difficult and volatile situation without resorting to force and violence. They solved that problem because of their resolve. Of course, it is not over. The strikes will be called off sooner or later, but people will have to live with the fact that strikes are a part of Polish life. Still, they no longer pose a threat to stability of the system in Poland. That was the main victory of her government. If she can maintain this kind of resolve, I am very optimistic.

I think that the most encouraging signs are in the economy as a whole. For the first time since the reforms began, the GNP has begun to grow slightly. Everyone agreed that the reforms would cause an initial drop in GNP, like pruning a tree and cutting off the deadwood. For instance, under the old system even if a factory was producing tanks no one wanted to buy, it would still produce them. The steel mills produced steel for them, and the engine factories produced engines. The productivity was great, but the tanks stood in the factory yard, and no one bought them. That type of unwanted production, not only in the field of armaments, but in other fields as well, had to be eliminated, which led inevitably to recession.

The idea behind the whole reform program was that after a certain period of time, the economy would be more market-oriented and productivity would grow. I think that moment is being witnessed now. Already the economy is on a new, sound basis and is steadily improving. It is still very risky because it has only been three months since this growth started, but it is an encouraging sign.

Another encouraging sign is that 52 percent of people employed in Poland are now employed in the private sector. It was crucial to privatize the economy by disposing of the state-owned factories and enterprises. The Polish people learned by bitter experience that the state can do many things, but it cannot produce anything except bureaucracy and regulations.

So, the question of privatization is tough, but with 52 percent employment, over 40 percent of GNP is now produced in the private sector. These signs are encouraging, because this private sector can cushion the effects of bankruptcies of the big state enterprises. In east Germany, they simply closed down the whole ineffective state-owned industry, but the result was that the unemployment rate rose to 50 percent. Poland could not afford that kind of social upheaval. Therefore, it has to wait to close the ineffective factories until the private sector is strong enough to hire the people working there in order to have a smoother transition. There is also the question of how quick this transition should be. Poland is quoted as an example of "shock therapy." It was not as much of a shock as in Germany, but it was still quite fast.

I think that this shock therapy was the only choice possible, because if you want to change the system, you have to crush it. There are always vested interests—people living off a certain system who will fight to preserve it. The cries in Poland for "industrial policy," and demands that the state not abandon its workers are simply cries to return to the system where the state provided jobs, social security, and everything. If you do not crush the old system all at once, it will become very difficult to deal with. An example of vested interests is Russia, where they were not strong enough to crush the whole system. The reforms did not take hold because there is still excess creation of money to subsidize ineffective factories, and the system that went bankrupt in Poland is still bankrupt there. They hope to get some help from the West, but you cannot run a country as big as Russia on subsidies from the United States. I think the Polish approach was best, and I hope that if these current signs of recovery continue, maybe shock therapy will be the answer to those asking what kind of reform is best for the post-Communist world.

QUESTION: Americans are well aware that the small private sector in Poland has progressed remarkably well, but they have the impression that the heavy industry is resisting any kind of privatization or giving up the privileges they had secured in the past. Would you give us an idea of the mentality of the managerial class in Poland and how much power they wield, vis-à-vis the political efforts to privatize?

MR. KOZLOWSKI: There are two managerial classes. One is the old managerial class, made up of former managers of communist industry who lived in a system where the best managers were people with good connections in Warsaw, and who went there to get subsidies, raw materials, and markets for their goods. It was not done in a market-oriented economy, however. They were not looking for places to market their goods, or the best supplier for raw materials or spare parts. They simply went to the ministry to bargain and get the best deal. That class of managers strongly opposed the reforms, of course. Those managers now cry for an industrial policy, which in my understanding, is merely another phrase for returning to the old system.

There is also a growing new managerial class comprised of people who simply started their own businesses. They are mostly in the trades and small businesses, not heavy industry. The history of the economy shows us that industry always started with trade. If you have private trade, the tradesman will demand goods and will need someone to manufacture them.

The crucial problem is capital. To build something, you need capital, and that is why Poland is desperately trying to lure foreign investment in, albeit without much success yet. Hungary and Czechoslovakia are doing much better in that respect. In 1991, Poland had about $1 billion in total foreign investment. Hungary, which has about one-fourth our population, had about $2 billion foreign investment in 1991.

I think the reason for this difference is the amount of red tape in Poland that scares some investors. There is also the unstable political situation. I think the situation is changing now that some big companies from the United States and other countries are coming. There is a possible deal where General Motors would take over a second car factory and produce Opels. By the way, GM in Europe is very profitable. Poland already has a big investment from Coca-Cola. One of Poland's bankrupt aircraft factories now has a deal to produce doors for Boeing Aircraft.

So, investment is coming at a much slower pace than the Polish people would wish, but it is coming. A big change will be the mass privatization plan, which is now being considered by parliament. I hope parliament will pass the plan and thus start the process of privatizing 600 big factories overnight. It is a complicated system. People will receive vouchers that will be invested in mutual funds. The mutual funds will manage these privatized factories. A problem of all post-Communist countries is how to create capitalism without capital overnight. The United

States had 200 years to do that. Poland has had approximately two years.

QUESTION: A great deal of foreign aid is available to Poland. How much of that foreign aid helps support state-owned industrial companies, and how effective is the leverage of that foreign aid in privatization and obtaining matching funds?

MR. KOZLOWSKI: There is indeed a lot of foreign aid, especially from the United States. About $400 million of foreign assistance goes to Poland. Poland was the most advanced, and therefore, the first to be noticed for this assistance. This assistance is important and the Polish people welcome it, but they have to be realistic. No matter how much assistance comes, it will not change the economic system. Germany is the best example. You cannot change the economic system in a country with foreign donations. It simply cannot work. The success or failure of reform will be fought out on the battleground in Poland. Assistance is important, but cannot solve everything.

COMMENT: I happened to be privileged to know of a transaction in which a company was prepared to take all of the risks, put up all of the money for an investment project in Poland, but it was turned down. It appears there is some evidence that they are perpetuating the state-owned industrial complex.

MR. KOZLOWSKI: Vested interests, as I said.

QUESTION: Do I understand correctly that the figure of 52 percent now employed in the private sector includes agriculture, which was private before the fall of communism?

MR. KOZLOWSKI: Yes, about 20 percent are in agriculture and the other 32 percent are in other sectors.

QUESTION: To what extent do you see the transformations taking place outside of Warsaw? Ultimately the impact of the reforms on your political parties and your economy depends on the transfer of this modernization-changeover process into the local areas. How is that developing?

MR. KOZLOWSKI: Big cities like Kraków, Poznań, and Gdańsk are on the forefront of reform. Things are changing very quickly. The question is, how deep does it go? I heard from a friend of mine who spent two months traveling in Poland. He said that for the first time, he had seen some real changes in the smaller places as well. This change means entrepreneurial spirit. People are starting up businesses. The reform, however, is to a great extent geographically divided, and the situation is worse on the "Eastern Wall." The eastern part of Poland was historically more backward, along with the former Soviet Union. The current overall unemployment rate is 13 percent, but the unemployment in the small towns in eastern Poland is as high as 40 percent. The further west you go, the better the situation is.

It is strange how historical factors play a role. For instance, the Poznań region, which was under German rule before World War I, is still the most advanced economically. There the reform is the most successful. The eastern region is in much worse shape, however.

QUESTION: I take it from the tenor of your comments that you believe the multifarious political parties are likely to continue to be stable enough to provide support for a parliamentary government that will be able to hold things together and keep this program moving along.

MR. KOZLOWSKI: Yes, that is exactly my hope, and I base it on the developments of the last three months. The crisis in June, when the Olszewski government was voted out of office, showed that this fragmented parliament was quarreling and in trouble. There was even talk of some possibility of a coup d'etat then. I think that this parliament looked down into the abyss and saw that if they continued their infighting, it might bring disastrous results. Therefore, they set aside their daily quarrels and voted the former government out with a sound majority of 270 votes. They voted in the new government with the same sound majority. Afterward, there were good examples of parliamentary cooperation in June, and important laws were passed. Parliament then went into recess. They reconvened last week and are going to discuss the mass privatization law, which will be the most crucial economic law to be passed. If they pass that law—that test—as I hope they do, the situation will improve.

This popular support for the Suchocka government is encouraging. If you want to win the next election, you have to feel what people are saying. If parliamentarians go against the government, they will lose the support of future voters.

QUESTION: What was the population of Poland in 1945, at the end of World War II? What is it now? How many people were lost in World War II?

MR. KOZLOWSKI: At the end of World War II Poland changed its frontiers and was shifted from the east to the west, so it is difficult to give an exact population number. Many Poles living in the east were moved west, and many Germans living in Poland were expelled to Germany. Altogether, Poland had 35 million people in 1939. About 6 million people—the Jewish population was 3.5 million people—were lost during World War II. In 1945, there were 29 million people, and now there are nearly 40 million. That is the demographic data.

QUESTION: Germans and Bulgarians tried to punish the Communists. In Poland and Hungary, I have not heard of any Communists being tried and sentenced. Shouldn't they be?

MR. KOZLOWSKI: Many people are furious to see the former Communists in positions of power, which is understandable. The problem is how to deal with that in practical terms. Who is to decide in a democratic society who should be removed from office? You cannot have a witch hunt. If you want to have a legal state, you cannot simply dismiss someone just because you do not like him. Now our parliament is tackling the de-communization law. I think it is a nightmare.

I would not like the former Communist jailers to be discharged en masse, because someone has to watch the prisoners. If the jailers were fired who years ago kept the political opposition in prison (such as me), who would keep the robbers and the thieves in jail now?

Getting rid of people in a legal way is extremely difficult. Many of these people were not committing crimes. Some did, and these people should be brought to justice. Being a Communist apparatchik, however, was not a crime at that time. If you want to have a lawful society in the future, how can you bring these people to justice now when they did not commit any crime?

Starting with that kind of witch hunt opens up a terrible possibility for private vendettas. Historical revolutions show that if you start a witch hunt, you never know where to stop. First you will get the real Communists, the big apparatchiks, but then you go further. If you start that kind of machine, it is very hard to stop.

QUESTION: I was wondering whether any particularly strong individuals are emerging who appeal to discontented people by encouraging scapegoating, and who might then coalesce into a strong opposition with less than democratic intentions?

MR. KOZLOWSKI: That is a real threat and was a possibility in this June crisis. There was talk about a possibility of a coup d'etat in the government in the wake of the disclosure of secret police files. If you decide who is eligible to run for parliament and who is not on the basis of information contained in those files, that leads to a very dangerous situation.

Former Nazi Germany is often cited as an example Poland should follow in de-communization. The only difference is that Poland does not have the American army to help it. You can attempt that kind of purge only if you have an external force—someone who is not personally involved. Everyone in Poland, in one way or another, had to deal with the former system. You could be in the opposition, but you were still dealing with the system—sending children to the Communist state school, working in the state factory, buying in the state shop. Everyone working was somehow involved. To draw the line between the just and the unjust, only God can do that—not human beings.

NARRATOR: You have dealt with large and difficult issues. Those of us who were involved with the de-Nazification process in Germany know exactly how difficult some of that was, even as late as the 1950s with the education program. You have helped us understand the situation in Poland, and we thank you very much.

III.

CONSTITUTIONS AND ELECTIONS

The Polish Interim Constitution of 17 October 1992: The Executive and the Elections*

LESZEK GARLICKI

NARRATOR: Professor Garlicki has spoken here on at least two other occasions and attended conferences at the University of Virginia. He is a member of the faculty of law at the University of Warsaw and has taught at numerous American universities: Capital University, the University of Indiana, and a number of others. Mr. Garlicki has written widely on the subjects of Polish constitutions and Polish law, but he has also written about our Supreme Court and compared Polish laws to the constitutions of other countries. He was an adviser to a subsection of the Roundtable, which played a leading role in the transition to democratic government in Poland.

Mr. Garlicki will not speak exclusively on the most recent Polish elections, but he will include them in his discussion on the Polish executive and other changes in the Polish government. We welcome him back to the Miller Center.

MR. GARLICKI: It is an honor to be here and present some of my observations and conclusions concerning Poland and the problems in Polish political life.

As usual, Polish politics is currently complicated. I was here in May 1992, just two or three days before the fall of the Olszewski

---

Presented in a Forum at the Miller Center of Public Affairs on 30 September 1993.

government. I remember that I was somewhat pessimistic, and some people were angry at me, but I was right. I had very good reasons to be pessimistic about the government of Mr. Olszewski.

Today, the situation is once again complicated. Poland recently had its parliamentary elections, and it is in the process of forming a new cabinet. It is impossible to predict how long it will take and what the outcome will be, so I am quite torn about my obligations. My presentation today will be about the developments in the Polish executive branch and its existing problems, which include elections.

In Poland, a weak presidency was built into the constitution of 1921, the so-called March Constitution. This constitutionally weak presidency was filled by a strong political leader, Mr. Józef Piłsudski, against whom the constitution was made. Nevertheless, Piłsudski was able to seize power in 1926.

The next constitution, the constitution of 1935, provided a strong presidency, but a leader that was strong enough for this constitution no longer existed (Piłsudski died in May 1935). As a result, Poland had a constitutionally strong presidency but weak leadership.

After the Second World War, there was no president at all under the constitution of 1952. The first secretary of the Communist Party, however, was more than a president. He was clearly the head of the state, or the head of the entire governmental system.

Thus, at different times there were different motives behind the constitutions. Moreover, constitutions were often written for specific people. The problem, however, was that by the time the constitutions were finally official, the next generation of politicians could already be in power. As a result, the constitutional texts and personal abilities were sometimes not compatible. My feeling is that after 1989 several similar situations in Poland can be observed.

What was the starting point? What was the situation in 1989? Poland still had the constitution adopted in 1952, a typical Communist constitution for an East European country. There were at least two important features of the 1952 constitution. First, this constitution was written with the full knowledge that it would not be observed or enforced. The founding fathers of this constitution had no illusions—it was just written for the sake of appearance. It was not meant to be a legal document and could not be applied in political reality; thus, they could write down everything they wanted. There were no legal constraints in writing the constitution because there was no court; there was no way to enforce what was written in the constitution.

Second, the constitution adopted the principle of unity of state power. This principle means that the constitution declared that the whole state apparatus was organized like a pyramid with a Parliament on the top and all other state agencies or branches of government subordinate to the Parliament. Of course, this arrangement was not practiced in reality.

In 1988 and 1989, the Communist Party suddenly discovered that the idea of a constitution was not stupid. There might be some reason to have a constitution that must be observed. This shift was, of course, due to political changes that deprived the Communist Party of its absolute hold of power. It began to look for a constitution with supplementary guarantees for the party's survival.

This concern was the source of the so-called April Amendment, which was adopted in April 1989 as a direct result of the Roundtable talks between Solidarity and the Polish Communist Party. There were three main effects of the Roundtable talks, at least as far as the constitution and politics are concerned.

First, Solidarity was restored to legality. Second, parliamentary elections were held and Solidarity was invited to participate. Solidarity, however, was allowed a maximum of only 35 percent of the seats in the most important chamber of the Parliament—the *Sejm*. The elections were only partly democratic (since the general proportions of the distribution of seats were already known), but Solidarity was nevertheless present in the Parliament as the opposition. Third, as a constitutional prize for this new composition of the Parliament, a new strong presidency was established in Poland. These decisions were made by the Roundtable in April 1989, and the old Parliament immediately adopted a constitutional amendment introducing the new presidency. At that time, the Communist Party logically believed that it would survive and Jaruzelski would be president.

From the constitutional point of view, this pyramid system with the Parliament on top was disrupted by introducing the powerful presidency. The president, by definition, had to be very strong and had to be anti-parliamentarian for political reasons. The presidency was given to General Jaruzelski, and he was understood to be a guarantee against the Parliament, even if Solidarity was only a minority, making any stupid decisions—from the perspective of the Communist Party, that is. Thus, the president was given formidable powers, mostly to curb the Parliament if necessary.

Under the April Amendment of 1989, the president was to be elected by the National Assembly (the two chambers of Parliament sitting together). This provision did not fit the anti-parliamentarian character of the presidency, but it was agreed that the presidency would be given to Jaruzelski. It would have been rather difficult to introduce a system in which the president was popularly elected and have Jaruzelski elected. Thus, a compromise was necessary.

All other elements of the presidential position were more typical. The president was accountable to the Parliament only in a procedure of impeachment. The procedure was complicated, with a two-thirds majority required to impeach the president, which was practically impossible to achieve. Also, presidential acts did not require a countersignature by a member of the cabinet. As a result, there was no cabinet responsibility for presidential actions, as well as a limited possibility of impeachment of the president.

The amendment was vague in describing what duties the president should have. The constitution stated that the president watches over the implementation of the constitution, secures the state's independence and its internal security, and secures adherence to Poland's international agreements and military treaties. These clauses were very general and gave the president undefined powers.

What does it mean to watch over the implementation or the observation of the constitution, to ensure that international treaties are fulfilled, and to secure the independence and internal security of Poland? It did not mean anything, but great potential for interpretation was present in a serious situation. It would be easy for the president to take actions claiming that they were part of his constitutional duty and within his presidential rights. Additionally, the idea existed that the president should be given powers allowing him to intervene when necessary.

The president had strong powers over the Parliament. First, he had the power of legislative veto. The veto could be overruled, but it required a two-thirds majority, which was very difficult to obtain. In addition, the president had the power to dissolve Parliament in certain enumerated cases. One such case was if the Parliament made a decision or adopted a law that could make it impossible for the president to exercise his constitutional duties. Other possibilities for use of presidential power over the Parliament also existed. For example, if the Parliament does not nominate a cabinet during its first three months, the president can dissolve the Parliament.

As far as the cabinet is concerned, however, there were some gaps in its construction. The April Amendment gave the president the exclusive power to nominate the prime minister and the rest of the cabinet, but it still did not totally overrule the pyramid idea. The power of final appointment of the cabinet continued to be a power of Parliament. In short, the president had a monopoly on proposals, but the Parliament had a monopoly on appointments. If the Parliament did not adopt any presidential proposals, however, it could be dissolved after three months. Also, only the Parliament had the power to dismiss the cabinet by a vote of no-confidence. The president was therefore strong but also had certain constraints. The presidency was designed with some special situations in mind, such as states of emergency and military interventions, and not just the normal daily activities of the government.

Parliamentary elections were held in June 1989, and in July Jaruzelski was elected as president of Poland. Almost immediately after the parliamentary elections, the whole system collapsed. The results gave Solidarity the ability to form the cabinet—the Mazowiecki cabinet in August 1989.

One has to give credit to Jaruzelski because he practically withdrew from his constitutional role. He remained president for the next year, but except for one or two situations, he did not exercise his presidential powers. The result was the gradual parliamentarization of the system. For the Solidarity government of Mr. Mazowiecki, its main partner was now the Solidarity-led majority in the Parliament. The relations between the cabinet and the Parliament soon began to remind one of the so-called second

Polish republic under the constitution of 1921—a parliamentary cabinet supported by a parliamentary majority. It became more and more clear that the president was a decorative personality who did not want to intervene even if he could; that is, although the president's powers were so formidable that if he wanted to intervene he would have had many different possibilities, he chose not to.

In September 1990, the so-called September Amendment was adopted. It called for the election of the president by popular vote. As a consequence, in December 1990 Walesa was elected president, and the last vestiges of the Roundtable talks and Jaruzelski's team were removed together.

The next cabinet, chaired by Mr. Bielecki, was a cabinet that had both some confidence of the president and some support of the parliamentary majority. Once again the system began to function more like a parliamentary system than a presidential system. Bielecki's government cooperated quite well with the Solidarity group in the Parliament, although not without some problems. Walesa was still trying to find out exactly what his constitutional position was. No serious conflicts between the cabinet and the Parliament occurred, so again the president faced neither the opportunity nor the temptation to use or to abuse his constitutional powers. The system remained like a parliamentary system even though the letter of the constitution suggested a completely different setting.

The situation began to change in the fall of 1991. The October 1991 parliamentary elections were the first fully democratic elections after the transformation. Unfortunately, they were a bit too democratic. The election results brought 29 parties or groups into Parliament, and Parliament became hopelessly divided and fragmented. The strongest group, the Democratic Union of Mr. Mazowiecki, had less than 15 percent of the seats in the lower house of Parliament. In 1991 the Democratic Union had 62 seats; SLD, the post-Communist Party, had 60 seats; PSL, the Peasant Party, had 48 seats. The remaining seats were scattered among other smaller and bigger groups.

The result was an inability to form a lasting coalition that would work. Mr. Olszewski then formed an alliance of the center right political parties and was finally able to form a cabinet. From the beginning, however, many sources of tension were present on both sides. Olszewski's cabinet was barely a majority cabinet—most in the Parliament were against him or just tolerated him for other reasons. More important, numerous sources of tension also existed between the president and the prime minister. Olszewski and Walesa had contradictory opinions from the beginning, especially as far as the direction of military forces and other sensitive problems in the functioning of the state were concerned.

The president won in a clever way. He helped provoke a parliamentary crisis, the so-called Lustration Crisis, which arose upon the disclosure of some alleged secret service files demonstrating that many Parliamentarians, the speaker included, had collaborated with the Communist secret service. The Lustration Crisis contributed to the Parliament's vote of no-confidence in Olszewski. The president was behind the scenes, of course, but the Parliament registered the vote of no-confidence and dismissed the Olszewski cabinet. Constitutionally, this vote of no-confidence was the next step in the parliamentarization of the system. It was a typical situation in a parliamentary system. The Parliament dismissed the cabinet.

Then the Suchocka cabinet emerged, a cabinet again led by the Democratic Union. At this moment it was already more or less clear that it was impossible to continue to live under both the April Amendment and the 1952 Constitution. Too many gaps, loopholes, and constitutional problems were present. It led finally to the adoption of the so-called Small Constitution. Poland at that time still did not have a new complete, comprehensive constitution. The "Small Constitution" contained an interim constitutional act regulating the relations between the executive and legislative branches. It was adopted on 17 October 1992 and introduced a version of "rationalized parliamentarianism." This system is basically parliamentary and gives a great deal of power to the Parliament, but at the same time it has several other procedures or institutions in case the Parliament is unable to exercise its constitutional duties.

The system of the Small Constitution presently enforced in Poland has two different "faces" depending on one crucial factor: the existence of a stable majority in Parliament. If a stable majority is present in Parliament, the Parliament is a dominant force within the state machinery. If no stable majority exists in the Parliament, then the president begins to exercise his constitutional role. It is not that the powers of the Parliament are given to the president. The question is who controls the cabinet, or rather, the government. If there is a stable majority within the Parliament, it is able to nominate the cabinet. Thus, Poland has a parliamentary cabinet, and whether or not the president is happy with this cabinet does not matter. When no parliamentary majority exists to nominate a cabinet, the president nominates the cabinet, and thus Poland then has a presidential cabinet. This cabinet becomes more or less subordinate to the president, not the Parliament. At this moment the president, together with the cabinet, has the constitutional potential to be quite strong.

In examining these constitutional provisions more closely, we find that the constitutional clauses about the president did not change much. The president is still chosen by a popular election and has limited responsibility as far as impeachment is concerned— only a two-thirds majority in the National Assembly can impeach the president, which is difficult. The requirement of counter-signature, however, has been revived. Most presidential acts must now be countersigned by the prime minister or by the relevant minister. If a presidential cabinet is in power, ministers would likely countersign any act promoted by the president. But when a parliamentary cabinet is in power, obtaining countersignature could be difficult, thus hindering the president's ability to exercise many of his powers. This requirement is one of the new elements in the Small Constitution.

The president still has undefined powers as far as his general duties are concerned. He still watches over the implementation of the constitution, ensures implementation of international treaties, and secures the internal and external security and independence of the state. The president retains the powers he had under the April Amendment, which leaves a great deal of potential presidential power.

The president still has the ability to dissolve the Parliament, but only in three situations: when the Parliament fails to adopt a state budget, fails to nominate or to accept a cabinet, and expresses a vote of no-confidence against the existing cabinet and does not appoint another cabinet.

The process of cabinet formation and cabinet responsibility is probably one of the most important elements of the Small Constitution. First, the cabinet is appointed by the president. The president designates a prime minister, who then proposes to the president to appoint the cabinet. From this moment, the cabinet legally exists.

This cabinet has to be accepted by the Parliament in 14 days. If there are not enough votes in Parliament to confirm this cabinet, the Parliament has the power to appoint its own cabinet by a majority vote. If no majority exists in the Parliament, the president can try it again. The Parliament can also try again, but in the end, the president has the option to dissolve the Parliament or nominate his own presidential cabinet for six months. If the Parliament fails to confirm any cabinet after six months, the Parliament must be dissolved. In practice, therefore, once the Parliament fails to nominate its own cabinet and the president nominates a cabinet, the presidential cabinet could always exist. It could function once as a full power cabinet and once as an acting or interim cabinet. Nevertheless, as long as the Parliament fails to produce a cabinet, the presidential cabinet can continue in office.

A similar situation occurs concerning the cabinet's accountability. The Parliament has the power to express a vote of no-confidence against the government (i.e., the cabinet). After a vote of no-confidence, there are two possibilities. The first possibility is a "simple" no-confidence vote where the Parliament simply has a vote of no-confidence against the cabinet. Then the president has two options: to accept the vote of the Parliament, dismiss the cabinet, and nominate a new cabinet; or to dissolve the parliament. When the president was confronted with such a symbolic vote of no-confidence in May 1993, he decided to take the side of the Suchocka government and dissolve the parliament.

The second type of vote of no-confidence is called the "constructive" vote of no-confidence. In this case, the Parliament expresses its vote of no-confidence and simultaneously nominates a new prime minister. The president is then bound by this decision, and the Parliament cannot be dissolved. It demonstrates once again that the whole system of the Small Constitution is built on the idea of reward and punishment. As long as a majority exists in the Parliament, the Parliament is rewarded and allowed to have its own cabinet and introduce any changes in this cabinet. The president has very limited avenues to fight against the Parliament in this case. The use of veto power is possible, but even the veto can be over-ruled. Once there is no longer a majority over 50 percent, however, the Parliament is punished. The cabinet shifts to the president, who can then control the whole executive branch. This situation leaves the president numerous possibilities, except legislation, to control the government.

In May 1993, the Parliament was dissolved. In September 1993, parliamentary elections were held. Thus, the first experience with the Small Constitution has occurred, but at the same time, September 1993 may mark another important date in the consti-tutional history of Poland. Why?

When the Small Constitution was adopted in the fall of 1992, the Parliament was fragmented. Responding to the situation, the president, accepting the Small Constitution, had in mind this system of punishment and rewards. He thought the Small Constitution could be used against him, but because the Parliament was not strong enough, he believed he would be able to control the develop-ments concerning the legislative and executive branches. As long as the Parliament was fragmented, the very existence of the Suchocka government depended on the president and his ability to dissolve the Parliament, which proved that the president is a very powerful figure.

Since the latest parliamentary elections, however, it is possible that a strong majority will form in the Parliament. Suddenly, the president could be confronted with a surprise. The Small Consti-tution is still the same, but the existing Parliament raises the possibility for a completely different version of the situation. Once a strong majority exists in Parliament, the president may have prob-lems controlling the operation of both the executive and legislative branches.

These changes lead to the question of elections—their signifi-cance and possible political results. It is very difficult to predict

anything in Poland and a risky undertaking, but I can at least pose some questions.

First, who lost? Who won? Who survived the elections? It is clear that the Catholic parties and other parties that formed the right wing in Poland lost. The only right-wing party that got into Parliament was the Confederation for an Independent Poland, led by Mr. Moczulski. With only 22 seats in the *Sejm*, however, even their presence is symbolic. Maybe it could rescue a cabinet in some combination of parliamentary seats, but that possibility is doubtful. All remaining right-wing or center-right parties lost and are not represented in the Parliament.

Neither is the only Polish neo-Nazi party represented in Parliament. This party received a total of 14,000 votes, which is not very impressive. They had a chance to run in the elections, but their support was not very impressive. This lack of support is good news.

Who else lost the elections? To some extent, the Democratic Union lost. It received only 74 seats in Parliament. While that is more seats than last time, it is still nothing compared to other parties. Whether the president lost the elections or not is the next question. Before the elections, the president established the Non-Partisan Bloc for the Support of Reform—BBWR. This bloc received only 16 seats in Parliament (less than the president wanted), but they are nevertheless—as the only "new" party—present in Parliament.

The Left won this election. It is clearly visible that the Democratic Left Alliance, or the post-Communist Party, won the elections with 171 seats, even more than in the first Parliament in 1989 when the election was partially predetermined. The Polish Peasant Party, which also has some close ties with a party from the Communist era, received 132 seats. The Union of Labor, another left party, was in fourth place with 41 seats. The success of the left wing was apparent.

Survivors of the election included the Democratic Union, the president's bloc (the BBWR), and the Confederation for an Independent Poland. This outcome is very good because the presidential group and the Confederation for an Independent Poland are in Parliament. The problem is that the other opposition groups are not present in Parliament. This could easily lead to a phenomenon of so-called outside-parliamentary opposition. If too many parties and political orientations are not represented, the Parliament will cease to be representative and will begin to lose its legitimacy. It would then be easy to attack Parliament. The current Russian Parliament, which is described as representing just one political orientation and thus easy to attack politically, is an example. The presence of the president's bloc and the right-wing Confederation for an Independent Poland at least gives some illusion that the Parliament is representative.

Another question that has arisen upon the election results is, will Poland go back to communism? Of course, that is the first impression. If the numbers of the SLD (the post-Communist Democratic Left Alliance) and the PSL (the Peasant Party) are combined, they have almost a two-thirds majority. It is not that simple, however. First, it is not likely that these two parties will form a durable coalition. The Peasant Party now represents another special interest—farmers and other agricultural interests—which are in clear conflict with the interests of industrial trade unions and other groups that voted for the Democratic Left Alliance. Thus, a coalition is possible numerically, but it would be unlikely to survive. A coalition would also be risky from a political point of view because it would create a bad international impression. The Communist rule of Poland would be clearly demonstrated.

Where are the Communists? There is the post-Communist Party, as it is described, but there are few Communists in it. My theory is that the last real Polish Communists were probably shot in the Soviet Union in 1937. Since then, finding Communists in Poland has been difficult. My feeling is that what was called communism in Poland was a nice description for the domination of the imperial politics of the Soviet Union over Poland and Eastern Europe. As long as the Soviet Union existed, the Communist Party in Poland had to exist to implement Soviet domination over Eastern Europe and Poland.

Now the international situation has changed, and the Polish Communists—or post-Communists—are far even from their recent roots. A new generation has emerged, and it is possible that this party represents other political interests. The post-Communist

Party is involved in many different business enterprises and ventures. Real communism is probably the last thing they have in mind.

This leads us to wonder how much room for action any new coalition would have. There are at least four potential adversaries or forces that the new coalitions will have to face. The first adversaries are the right-wing parties and their electorates, who would be in strong opposition to a left coalition. There is no way to find a compromise solution between them, but let's assume that it could be done.

The second important force that has to somehow be accommodated is the Catholic Church. The Catholic Party lost in the election, but the Church, of course, is very strong. The question now is, to what extent could any possible coalition or coalitions confront the Catholic Church? Or, to what extent would a coalition with the participation of the post-Communist Party rather continue the traditional politics of the Polish Communists just to appease the Church, or look for a deal with the Catholic Church? The problem of ratification of the recent treaty with the Vatican, the Concordat, rests on the issue of abortion. This factor could be important in contemplating how much room for action there is for a coalition.

The third force is the Solidarity Trade Union, which still exists, although it also lost in the election. It is now possible that Solidarity, being dissatisfied with the results of the election, would organize another action—a strike for social demands, like those that were carried out by the post-Communist trade unions under the rule of the Democratic Union. These actions could be dangerous because they could increase the social pressure on the budget policies of the new cabinet.

Finally, is the president able or willing to support any of these coalitions? How can the president be appeased and brought to the side of this new coalition? These are important questions. It is not inconceivable that any of these combinations would have to involve or take into account the wishes of the president. Regardless of the text of the constitution and the majority in Parliament, the real power of the president could still be very important in the possibilities for the acceptance of the cabinet.

The most difficult challenge that faces the new cabinet are the social demands. The campaigns for the elections were run under the following promises: the economic situation would change; social benefits as they now exist could be kept; jobs would be kept; the ruin of Polish agriculture by imported goods from Western Europe would be stopped, and so on. All of these promises, if taken seriously (I hope they will not be taken too seriously by the new coalition) can immediately incite inflationary processes and again cause some dangerous economic situations in Poland. Most of these possible coalition partners, however, probably know that being in the cabinet means being accountable to the voters for electoral promises.

I do not know what the outcome will be, as there several different possibilities and ideas. Not everything in politics is reasonable; things can have unreasonable solutions.

Again, I do not believe a durable coalition will result between the SLD and PSL, two of the biggest partners. Even if it could be formed for some time, eventually another coalition could be formed by the post-Communists (SLD). It probably would be a coalition either with the Union of Labor (UP) or maybe with the Democratic Union. It would be a difficult coalition for the Democratic Union, however. The resulting combination, however, is likely to be a shaky one, giving a great deal of power and many possibilities to the Peasant Party, the strongest group in this scenario. But the president just proposed his own candidate, even though his Non-Partisan Bloc for the Support of Reform is weak. He has a very good candidate, Andrzej Olechowski, who is respected in Poland as an expert in economics and could lead some kind of parliamentary or nonparliamentary government, or a political government of experts. The president could use him to avoid problems and tensions in the Parliament. Who knows, the Parliament might accept it. Currently, there is the Suchocka cabinet, and it will probably take weeks to form a new cabinet. Therefore, there may still be a little time to discuss, count, and produce some results. I understand that in two weeks there will be another presentation about these elections. Maybe by then something will have transpired.

QUESTION: What is your reaction to the wave of pessimism reflected in our press—that is, the conclusion that these results heralded the doom of free enterprise in Poland and that the country with the best chance for bringing about a free enterprise regime was now likely to have shaky economic development?

One economist had another point of view. He argued that policy had not been wrong, but too harsh, and that what had happened in Poland represented an effort to develop free enterprise too rapidly. In the English-speaking world, reactions of that kind are somewhat common. What is your reaction to the gloom and doom?

MR. GARLICKI: I think the initial reactions in Poland were also pessimistic, and most of the voters were afraid of what they had done. It is only the first look at these numbers that is so shocking. These people who know a great deal about Poland and who by no means are friends of the Communist Party have presented their more moderate positions.

Once more, there is probably no reason to panic. Any new coalition would also know that Poland was the only East European country that experienced some economic growth both last year and this year. Disrupting that growth by some premature fulfillment of social demands would bring a catastrophe in two or three years.

The only important question is whether the political parties in the new coalition are able to consider long-term effects. Two or three years is a long time in Poland. I am not pessimistic as far as the election results are concerned. On the other hand, I am concerned about the danger of premature or stupid actions being taken by the new coalition.

QUESTION: It has occurred to me that aside from the press reaction, this vote is almost a vote against the resulting crisis dimensions and the promises of big changes. It appears to be a vote in favor of more continuity or stability. I am not sure this will be the policy result, but many promises were made and many expectations were raised. Since 1989, people have actually been living in a fairly crisis-ridden situation. To me, the election results are certainly not a return to communism. As you said, communism was never a strong force ideologically in Poland. Could some call for stability and limited risk be one of the messages of the election results?

MR. GARLICKI: Yes, I think there are at least two clear messages and one unclear message from the election results. The clear message is a rebuke to the right-wing parties. These parties have been quarreling among themselves instead of proposing something positive to the voters. As a result, they were discarded. This message is very clear.

The other message is a negative message to the Democratic Union. Generally, the people were dissatisfied with the Democratic Union. The Democratic Union had made many promises and its actions were full of indecisiveness. Too few new faces for the electoral campaign were given and many different accusations were made, especially against the Liberal Party, which was closely connected to the Democratic Union. Generally speaking, the electorate was dissatisfied with the Democratic Union and the party got the message: You are too arrogant and too intellectual in your actions. If a party forgets about its electorate, how can it win? If someone is unemployed, he would of course vote for the party who promises to find him a job. I believe it was a vote for stability, but at the same time, I do not think it was a vote for a complete change of economic policy.

COMMENT: I can see people voting for the person who was their employer if they were out of work.

MR. GARLICKI: As a matter of fact, that would be the case, but the question is to what extent those people are now able to secure jobs. It is important to remember that the post-Communist Party is closely involved in different economic ventures. I will not comment on the legality or morality of this situation, but it is a capitalistic and middle-class party as far as its economic interests are concerned. In reference to the Marxist way of thinking, their economic situation is far from introducing any rapid changes. Rather, they are interested in maintaining Poland's slow but constant economic growth. The pressure of the electorate could be very strong, however. Local elections come next spring, and the post-Communist Party would like to win these elections, but in order to do so it has to show some achievements.

COMMENT: The dramatic change that occurred in voter support for the different parties between 1991 and 1993 is startling. When combined, the two parties with the most votes moved up to a commanding majority compared with their fragmentation in 1991.

MR. GARLICKI: Most important was a new electoral law adopted in 1993. The elections of 1993 were still proportional, but with several limitations. A particular limitation was that parties needed a minimum of 5 percent of the vote to enter Parliament while coalitions needed 8 percent of the vote. Different combinations resulted and votes were eliminated.

Do not forget that almost 25 to 26 percent of votes were given to parties that did not meet the 5 percent threshold. The result was that strong parties profited. The SLD received 20.41 percent of the votes and over 35 percent of the seats. The electoral system operates in this manner—the strong parties are privileged. Under the previous system, 20 percent of the votes meant about 22 or 25 percent of the seats. This is a big change, but all parliamentary parties in the former Parliament voted for this electoral law. Each of the parties hoped it would win. Some of them were wrong.

NARRATOR: Americans are very interested in what the Polish people think about Walesa as an executive leader. Roosevelt might well work with the kind of coalition and problem you have mentioned. According to the news here, the creation of Walesa's new party took away votes from the Democratic Union and represented a somewhat selfish effort on the part of the president. If I understand you correctly, you do not necessarily agree with that opinion. Nevertheless, the media has made many comments about the current prime minister, suggesting that she was weak. There have also been mixed comments in the media, contrasting earlier comments made about Walesa. Could you comment?

MR. GARLICKI: First, Walesa has no reason to like the Democratic Union. Mazowiecki was the one who ran against him during the presidential elections in 1990. Although relations between Ms. Suchocka and Mr. Walesa are not bad, the Democratic Union is no longer the party that is close to the president, which is probably not exclusively Walesa's fault.

Second, the president was not very successful in supporting his nonpartisan bloc. He has the 16 seats, but that is not much. The elimination of the right-wing parties, however, was a very important win for the president in this election. Since 1991, the right-wing party of Mr. Olszewski and other similar parties have been the main enemies of Walesa. They tried to impeach him and politically eliminate him through the Lustration Case. They brought many other actions against him. The left-oriented parties are the successors of parties that had been friendlier toward the president. Therefore, he could be quite satisfied with these results even if he would like to have more of his nonpartisan bloc representatives in the Parliament.

Finally, my personal opinion is that Walesa is a very strange person. Listening to Walesa speak or comparing different speeches, one's first impression is that he is a person who does not understand anything. At the same time, however, he is very effective politically. An examination of almost all developments in Poland after 1989 results in the realization that Walesa always knew how to solve problems and win conflicts, even during the last crisis—the dissolution of Parliament and the call for new elections. In my opinion, more credit than criticism goes to Walesa because he at least is clearly not a loser. He is very effective, so politically he is a strong personality.

NARRATOR: We have certainly had a creative look today at the elections in Poland and we are, as always, much indebted to Professor Garlicki. Thank you very much.

CHAPTER FIVE

The 1993 Elections in Poland*

KRZYSZTOF JASIEWICZ

NARRATOR: Krzysztof Jasiewicz is a professor of sociology at Washington and Lee University. He is, in a sense, the Theodore White of Polish politics. Theodore White wrote a series of studies about successive presidential elections. Professor Jasiewicz has written a series of parliamentary election studies—1985, 1989, 1990 (presidential), and 1991. Those who know him have often described him as one of the most effective lecturers of higher education, and he has a considerable following at Washington and Lee. In addition, he has lectured at other universities around the United States, including Harvard and Yale, and in a number of European countries—the Netherlands, Great Britain, and others. In every case, he is highly praised as a scholar and teacher.

Professor Jasiewicz was born in Piła, Poland. He received both his master's and doctorate in Warsaw. He is a research fellow at the Polish Academy of Sciences, Institute of Political Studies and is serving as vice president of the Polish Studies Association (USA). He has held numerous fellowships, such as the Mellon Research Fellowship at the Russian Research Center at Harvard and a fellowship at the Woodrow Wilson International Center.

Professor Jasiewicz has had a special interest in provincial and local people's councils and political representation in Poland. He has written on these subjects in numerous articles and books: *Social Roles of Councilors of the Provincial People's Councils* and a forth-

---

*Presented in a Forum at the Miller Center of Public Affairs on 8 October 1993.

coming book, *Why Did They Vote This Way?*, which discusses presidential elections.

MR. JASIEWICZ: I would like to begin by making some comments on the results of the recent elections in Poland on 19 September 1993. In comparison to the 1991 elections, the most interesting things about these recent Polish elections are the dynamics and the changes.

It is a good Anglo-Saxon tradition to begin a public lecture with some kind of paradox and later to comment on this paradox. I am in an unfortunate position because I could not make a choice of just one good paradox. There are too many paradoxes in these recent Polish elections. I will only mention a few of them.

The happenings in Poland approximately three weeks ago have been presented as a considerable victory of the post-Communist Left. Indeed, the post-Communist Democratic Left Alliance (SLD) collected twice as many votes as two years ago and, moreover, gained a lion's share of the seats in the Parliament. Presently, the Democratic Left Alliance is conducting negotiations on forming a coalition with two other parties. One party is the Polish Peasant Party, the successor of the United Peasant Party, which had been an ally of the Communists between 1949 and 1989. Thus, it is another post-Communist Party, or one that has its roots in the old regime.

The third party in these negotiations is the Union of Labor, which has its roots in Solidarity, but by all standards represents Solidarity's Left. In my opinion, it is a typical social democratic, Western European-style party. The Union of Labor in many ways is more leftist than the Democratic Left Alliance. On some issues it is ideologically more orthodox than the post-Communist Alliance, which tends to be more pragmatic. Overall, the election was a victory of the Left. There are no doubts about that evaluation, particularly if one looks at the distribution of the seats in Parliament.

The peculiarities of the new Polish electoral law—a 5 percent threshold for parties and an 8 percent threshold for coalitions—transformed a moderate victory on the level of votes into a huge victory on the level of seats. The stronger parties (and in this case the post-Communists were the stronger) gained a plurality of the vote. They gained many more seats than their proportionate share of the votes. About 35 percent of all votes were, in a sense, wasted. They went to the parties that did not achieve this 5 percent threshold and therefore are not represented in Parliament. So in terms of the number of seats in Parliament, this election is an impressive victory for the Left.

On the level of the number of votes, this election can be seen in a different way. The two post-Communist parties, the Democratic Left Alliance and the Polish Peasant Party together received about 35 percent of the votes, while post-Solidarity parties received about 47 percent of the votes. In short, the post-Solidarity parties altogether gained more votes than the post-Communist parties. This percentage is not translated into seats in Parliament because the Solidarity movement split into several factions. These factions competed against one another, and many of them did not make it into Parliament at all.

This election can also be viewed from another angle. Based on the data of the 1991 elections, I performed several analyses of the ideological profiles of particular parties. Several indicators were used in complicated statistical operations. According to this ideological profile, the Left achieved about 27 percent of the vote; the liberal Center and liberal Right (I am using the term *liberal* in the European context of laissez-faire liberals) together gained about 23 percent. The populists, which represent the demands for a very protective state but with limited traces of socialist ideology, tend to be more religious or more rightist and ideologically anti-Communist. They gained about 25 percent (I included the Trade Union Solidarity in this group). The nationalistic groups and the religious Right also got about 25 percent. Therefore, even when one discounts the distribution of seats in Parliament, the distribution of votes still reflects a shift to the Left at the ideological level. This shift, however, is not as spectacular as it seemed after examining the distribution of seats alone.

Nonetheless, the post-Communist Left was victorious. I would now like to focus on the reasons why after what seemed to be the ultimate defeat of communism in Eastern Europe, this resurgence of the post-Communist Left occurred in Poland. Why did the voters support these post-Communist parties? This victory is the child of one mother and at least seven fathers and was delivered by a midwife. I shall explain who these actors—the mother, seven fathers, and midwife—are.

The "mother" is the Democratic Left Alliance. This post-Communist coalition is the successor of the ruling party in the Communist system. The Social Democracy of the Republic of Poland was the core of this coalition composed also of post-Communist trade unions, some women's organizations, and other organizations and independents. The reason for their achievement was that they maintained unity. This alliance was able to stay united as a coalition despite serious ideological and political differences. The mechanism that explains why they remained united is similar to the one that explained the unity of such bodies as Solidarity in Poland or the Civic Forum in Czechoslovakia when they were still struggling with the Communists. This unity is due to something that I call "Triple F," or the "formidable foe factor." As long as there was a threat of communism resurging, Communists in power, or Communists negotiating over governmental control, Solidarity stayed united. After the defeat of the Communists, Solidarity split into several factions. The Communists were overwhelmed by Solidarity in 1990 in the presidential election, but they now maintain unity, while Solidarity does not.

Another factor explaining the post-Communists' success was that they were able to maintain surprisingly good public relations by presenting themselves to the public as something different than what they had been in the past, as a European-style social democratic party rather than the old Communists. They made the distinction quite consciously and on various levels. For instance, their leader, Aleksander Kwasniewski lost 40 pounds in about three months time in what he called his commitment to the cause of his party. This gesture was received very well by the public and the media. The party thinks in modern terms. They do not think in terms of the old Communist Party, but rather in terms of modern politics when things such as the appearance of the leader count very much. Above all, they were able to present themselves as true representatives of some groups in society that were hurt by the progress of economic reforms—in particular, the groups that were paid from the state budget. These groups are pensioners, teachers, health service workers, and so on. All of the services in Poland were nationalized under communism, and all of those people are still state employees.

The same is true about the workers in the typical socialist mammoth enterprises. These enterprises were not yet privatized. They were not competitive in the marketplace and were also subsidized by the state. These groups did not gain from Poland's transformation to a free-market economy. The buying power of their family budgets decreased rapidly with the increase of prices to the market level, and many of them feel threatened by the reforms. The Democratic Left Alliance was able to present itself to these groups as the only party that would speak in their behalf. It was, of course, not the only party using this kind of campaign appeal, but it was the party that the poor were more likely to trust. In short, the fact that the post-Communist Democratic Left Alliance was able to act in a modern way and was able to accept the rules of the game of democracy worked in its favor and contributed to its electoral success.

The first of those mysterious seven fathers is, to quote a phrase from the 1992 presidential elections in the United States, "It's the economy, stupid." I was approached by several American journalists before and after the elections and was asked how it was possible that in a country with the fastest growing economy in Europe, the government in power lost so badly in the election. I think that Poland has the fastest growing economy in Europe, with about 1 percent economic growth in 1992 and, according to some estimates, 5 percent economic growth in GNP in 1993. So what was wrong with the economy?

Well, statistics are a tricky business. You can pick up one number and say it means something, but there are other numbers that mean something different. It is relatively easy to achieve impressive economic growth if you begin from a low level. It is well known in the history of economics that the first few years of economic recovery or economic development are the easiest. The point of departure for Poland was actually a very low GNP per capita compared to other countries' standards. The Polish economy was in decline basically from 1978 through 1983, with some stabilization at a low level in the mid-1980s and another decline from

1988 to 1992. The recovery began in April 1992, but it gives more joy to economists and statisticians than to the people on the streets who do not see the outcome of this recovery yet.

Moreover, there are other statistics—for example, 15 percent unemployment. This economic recovery was achieved within the context of a rapidly polarizing society in which some people get richer and many others get poorer. Many of those who are classified as unemployed are not really unemployed. For instance, recent graduates from high school who have never even looked for jobs are directed to unemployment agencies. Nonetheless, this 15 percent is still 15 percent more than five years ago, and the number is still growing. There was a policy of full employment under communism. The unemployment problem is the reason that the economy worked against the government in power.

I should also add that the Solidarity governments (there were four Solidarity governments between 1989 and 1993) were all disastrous in terms of public relations. They were not able to present their programs to the public or to sell them to the public. They were satisfied with the fact that their programs were the right ones in their opinion. I agree with this assessment. I think that the Balcerowicz program for economic recovery, which was run by the Mazowiecki government and later by the Bielecki government and the Suchocka government, was the right program, but they were simply not able to mobilize popular support for this program. Again, they were not able to play by the rules of liberal democracy or pluralist democracy in which it is not enough to be right. You have to convince the voters that you are right, and they did not convince them.

The second "father," or I should say a "stepfather," was the European Community. Maybe I am overgeneralizing, but the West and the European Community in particular first expressed its joy over the end of communism in Poland and the rest of Eastern Europe but later erected protective barriers against products from Eastern Europe and Poland. These barriers have affected Poland. The Suchocka, Bielecki, and Mazowiecki governments were previously presenting the Balcerowicz program of economic recovery as a program of joining with Europe and the European Community. Poland is due to become a member of the European

Community sometime in the future and has already become an associate member. At the same time, the European Community is sending different kinds of messages—"maybe sometime in the future it wants Poland as a full member, but not now." Even if this kind of message was negative from an economic point of view, it was not very important. What does it mean if a foreign government imposes an embargo on Polish cherries? Is that embargo going to hurt the Polish economy very much? No. It is going to hurt some farmer who has cherry orchards, but who else would suffer? Is it going to change any thinking in the European market? Not at all. This jealousy does not count in the overall economy, but such cases continue to be highly publicized and make the front pages of newspapers. It is a message from the European Community saying that it does not want us or our cherries. As a result, the government that was presenting itself as promoting Polish membership in the European Community could not convince the people that it was the right way for Poland.

The economy was not the only factor in these elections. Voters do not make decisions based exclusively on economic issues. Ideological and religious issues also have a profound impact on the results of the elections, which brings us to another paradox.

The Roman Catholic Church in Poland contributed as probably no other institution except Solidarity to the fall of communism in Poland. This role cannot be denied. It is simply the historic truth. But the Roman Catholic Church in Poland also contributed greatly to the shift toward the Left and the shift toward the post-Communists as expressed in the last election, becoming the third "father" of their victory. The reason for this influence was because the church leaders aggressively "pursued their own agenda." Moreover, in the Parliament of 1991-93, this agenda was supported by a slight majority—about 52 to 55 percent of the deputies. This agenda, however, was rejected by about 60 to 80 percent of the population at large. The political elites were sticking with the church and the church agenda, again forgetting that the voters would one day scrutinize their actions. The church has pressed for changes in the Polish abortion law since the late 1950s. This law was one of the most liberal in Europe. The church basically demanded prohibition of abortions. The law that became effective in May 1992 and was passed a few months earlier basically forbids abortions. It allows for abortions only in the cases of incest and rape. It is very difficult even in such cases to obtain an abortion in Poland. The church also insisted that the law on electronic media in Poland should have a clause about the protection of Christian values, and the law passed with this provision. The church insisted on the teaching of religion in schools, which was initiated as a result.

On these issues, let me again stress that about 60 to 80 percent of the Polish electorate, depending on the specific issue, presented an opposite point of view. They were against further intrusion of the church into their public and private lives. They wanted Poland to be a secular state, and an overwhelming majority supported the separation of the state and the church. This cleavage between religious fundamentalism and secularism at a time when Europe is secular further contributed to the shift to the Left in Poland.

An examination of the election returns shows the fate of the Fatherland Catholic Election Committee. It achieved about 900,000 votes in 1993, while the parties that composed this coalition achieved altogether more than a million votes two years earlier. They were losers in terms of the actual number of votes. Their share of votes was actually even lower given the higher turnout. The turnout in the 1993 election was nine points higher than the 1991 election. They were losers also in the sense that they did not gain any seats in Parliament. The two parties (the Christian National Union and the Party of Christian Democrats) ran as a coalition, but they did not make it over the 8 percent threshold.

The upper house of the Parliament, the Senate, was also elected. The Senate was elected on a plurality electoral system as opposed to proportional representation. The senators from the Catholic organizations were outspoken, for instance, in favor of the antiabortion legislation. They lost badly in these elections. The widest cleavage in Polish society was between confessional fundamentalism and secularism. This influence of the Catholic church was much feared by the people, in some instances even more than economic issues.

The fourth "father" of this victory of the Left in the Polish election was the Right—in particular, the post-Solidarity rightist parties like the Center Alliance or the Coalition for the Republic. Their first error was to run on an anti-Communist ticket when most of the people were simply indifferent to the slogans of decommunization. These slogans pressed the idea that the former members of the Communist Party or former officials of the Communist Party should be forbidden from taking any public offices in Poland for a period of time. Similar legislation was introduced into the former Czechoslovakia a year and a half ago before the split. The former members of the Polish Communist Party felt threatened. Most of the two-and-a-half million of them do not regret the demise of the party and of communism in Poland. They were not ideologically motivated Communists and therefore are not that kind of Communists now. They simply saw this proposed legislation as a threat to them, possibly denying them good jobs in the future or introducing some other kind of prosecution. As a result, the Right's proposal mobilized them to vote for the post-Communist Party. The Right, in a sense, mobilized their counterpart's ranks instead of their own. It produced a boomerang effect.

Moreover, the post-Solidarity rightist parties were not able to accept the rules of the game. They were not able to understand that in order to gain control over the Parliament, they had to form a coalition and therefore increase their chances and run on the joint ticket. They did not split over any political or ideological issues. They were using precisely the same wording in their campaigns. They split purely because of the ambitions of their leaders. There were almost as many parties as leaders. Therefore, they lost and are not represented in Parliament. It is likely that they will be active as extra-parliamentary opposition groups.

The fifth "father" of this victory of the Left is the Democratic Union, the major party in the Suchocka government coalition and also the party of former Prime Minister Mazowiecki. In the opinion of the public, this party has been in power for four years (since 1989), a mistaken opinion because this party was in opposition to the Olszewski government in early 1992. Nonetheless, many remember that they were people somewhere at the top. The public also perceived them as quite arrogant and as not caring about the people on the streets.

I am engaging here in an exercise that is popular in Poland: Democratic Union bashing. Everyone says the Democratic Union is responsible for anything that went wrong in Poland. I am not of this opinion even if I am critical of the party.

Another paradox is that the Democratic Union in the 1993 elections received more votes than in the 1991 elections. They were able to mobilize more people to vote for them—about 100,000 more voters. It is simply their share of the vote that was smaller than two years ago. They are also gaining more seats in Parliament. Their major mistake, in my opinion, was that they did not take advantage of the electoral law. The electoral law was the same for all of the parties. The Communists understood that the Democratic Union could have taken advantage of this law. The Democratic Union's first mistake was that they supported this version of electoral law when it was accepted earlier this year. They should not have done so, because in comparison to the 1991 law, there were more electoral districts, so the districts were smaller. There were 52 instead of 37 districts. The smaller districts were created in the rural areas. The Democratic Union traditionally was weak in the rural areas; the Peasant Party was strong, and in some rural areas the Democratic Left Alliance was also strong. Therefore, the smaller electoral districts with only three or four seats gave an edge to stronger parties and discriminated against a third or fourth party in a given district purely because of mathematics. Such a party, even if it gained sometimes 20 or 20-plus percent of the popular vote in a given district, may not get a single seat in the district. This possible result is a so-called effective threshold in which the minimum number of votes or minimum set of votes to get one seat is much higher in smaller districts than in larger districts.

I know from the insiders that leaders of the Democratic Union were told: "Don't do it; don't accept this change. It is going to work against you and in favor of your enemies." They would not listen.

The fact that their leaders ran in the same district was another problem. They were not running against each other because this is a multiseat district. For instance, Suchocka and Mazowiecki could be elected from the same district. But the idea was that a popular leader in a given district would pull a bandwagon of supporters. If

90

you have 52 popular leaders, you distribute them to 52 districts. If you have 104, you can put two in each district. There are not this many popular leaders, however, even in the Democratic Union. The party is composed of quite popular people, possibly 10, 15, or 20, but not 52. What is the point of putting two very popular leaders, Mazowiecki and Suchocka, or Kuroń and Geremek, also very popular leaders, in the same district? The other leaders should run somewhere else, attracting votes in other districts. I do not understand their decisions.

But the major mistake of the Democratic Union was not forming a coalition with the Liberals. The constituents of the Liberal Democratic Congress and the Democratic Union in terms of their ideological and political profiles are almost identical. They are in favor of the same policies. There were no reasons to run on a separate ticket. They should be together in a coalition. The fact that they did not form a coalition hurt them because many people said that since they could not agree on a coalition, they were not going to vote for any of those parties. Moreover, the reformers were hurt because the Liberals did not make it into the Parliament. They received 4 percent of the popular vote, so they were 1 percent short of the 5 percent threshold. Had the Liberals joined in a coalition with the Democratic Union, this coalition would have gained about 110 or 120 seats in Parliament. Now the Democratic Union has only 74 seats and the Liberals have none.

Thus, just this one decision within the context of this particular law would have given the Democratic Union and the Liberals a much larger share of the parliamentary seats. Some insiders blame the Liberals for this result because some of the Liberal leaders were against this coalition. I blame the senior partner. I think the leaders of the Democratic Union should have done everything they could to convince the Liberals that the coalition was a necessity at this point.

The sixth "father" of the Left's victory is Solidarity, the Trade Union. The fact that Solidarity submitted the motion for the vote of no confidence in the Suchocka government is probably one of the greatest paradoxes. The Suchocka government fell by just one single vote in Parliament. The new elections were called, and Solidarity is not represented in the *Sejm*. Its main enemy, the

OPZZ, the post-Communist Trade Unions that are part of the Democratic Left Alliance, now have 61 of the SLD's seats in Parliament. So Solidarity, in a sense, first destroyed communism, revived it, and then helped the post-Communists obtain control over the Parliament while putting itself out of the Parliament. I need to stress again Solidarity's nine seats in the Senate. Solidarity will be represented in the upper chamber, but in the lower chamber it actually fell short by only 13,000 votes.

This story is sad because it shows how Solidarity was an all-encompassing social movement, protective to all weak groups and also struggling for democracy, but nevertheless shrank to a narrow, radical group representing basically the anti-reform interests of some workers in Poland.

The seventh "father" is Lech Walesa, the president of Poland. I do not mean here his idea to create Nonparty Block to Support Reforms (BBWR), which was meant to be his political party. The BBWR probably will not become his political party because as he is not satisfied with only 5.4 percent of the popular vote, he will likely disassociate himself from this group, I believe.

The BBWR was not a bad idea. It allowed the representation of some pro-reform forces that otherwise would not have made it into the Parliament. At a certain point Walesa was seeking even a broader coalition. He wanted his party to run with the Democratic Union, the Liberals, and the Christian National Union as one coalition. This coalition, with some other parties, would have commanded enough votes to form a government and force the post-Communists into opposition. This was not a bad idea. I think things went wrong three years ago when during the electoral campaign Walesa called for this so-called war at the top—that is, competition among top Solidarity leaders, which led to the fragmentation of Solidarity. I am not saying that Solidarity would not have split without the war at the top called by Walesa. Solidarity was an all-encompassing movement comprised of people from several ideological and political orientations, but the nucleus of this consensus would have been preserved. We do not have this consensus anymore, and we will not have it anytime in the future. I think Walesa contributed greatly to the fragmentation of the

Solidarity movement and therefore to the strength of the post-Communists.

Now for the "midwife" of this scenario. As I mentioned, the motion of no-confidence in the Suchocka government passed by only one vote in the *Sejm*. Two deputies from the Christian National Union (at that time part of the ruling coalition) did not appear for the vote. Had just one of them come, the no-confidence motion would have been defeated. One of them was the former minister of justice who was fired by Suchocka. There was a rumor that he missed the vote intentionally to penalize Suchocka, but he does not admit to this action. He said that he was simply sick and could not make it on time. He arrived seven minutes late.

The real midwife of the post-Communist Left's victory was a deputy named Bogumita Boba. A doctor of medicine, she is a Catholic fundamentalist within the ranks of the Christian National Union. She perceived a coalition of the Christian National Union and Democratic Union as a betrayal of Catholic values. She saw the leaders of the Democratic Union as almost Communists and as people who are not committed to Catholic values. She announced about two days before the no-confidence vote that she would not participate in the vote because her values did not allow her to support a government led by Suchocka and the Democratic Union. On the other hand, she did not want to violate party discipline. Therefore, she simply did not appear for the vote.

The result is that the government in Poland now will be much more leftist than the Democratic Union could ever be accused of being. The law on abortion will probably be reversed or liberalized, and Dr. Boba will live in a much more secular state than she wanted. She also ran on the ticket of a fringe party and personally received about 1,000 votes in her district, which really is not worth mentioning, except that her case and the examples of Solidarity and the post-Solidarity rightist parties show that if you want a pluralistic democracy, you have to play by the rules of a pluralistic democracy and use these rules to your advantage. These people were the ones who called for democracy in Poland and the end of Communist rule, but they were also the ones who could not adjust to the new situation and the new rules of the game. Her case shows very clearly that in a pluralistic democracy, moderation and compromise are the ways to solve problems and are furthermore necessary if one is to be an effective politician. Radicalism or extremism of any sort does not work in one's favor, as in the case of Dr. Boba. The fringe parties and the populist parties—such as Party X—that were hoping to gain a tremendous number of votes as a result of popular dissatisfaction, followed a radical extremist program and consequently fared poorly in these elections.

In conclusion, I want to stress that even if there are political actors in Poland who do not really know their roles, what kind of play they are acting in, or what kind of game they are playing, they still comprise a democracy, especially in comparison to the situation in the former Soviet Union. The political and ideological problems in Poland are being solved by democratic means: by elections, negotiations, coalitions, and so on. They are not solved on the streets, and that fact provides an element of optimism in this generally pessimistic time.

NARRATOR: We have asked our colleague who is a member of the American Studies Program at the University of Warsaw to make a brief comment.

COMMENT: The elections were won by the post-Communist parties that have money. I was in Warsaw during the elections. Former Communist Party members had been gathering money and were just waiting for the right time. The Democratic Union is one of the richest political parties in Poland. The Peasant Party, which garnered 132 seats in Parliament, is also one of the most influential and richest parties in Poland.

Regarding the right-wing parties, I would say that they were completely unprepared for the elections. They did not care about the voters. They had no influence because they were not rich like the former Communists.

Indeed, the former Communists brought up the question of taxes, which is an important question in Poland because of the legal instability there. The former Communists blamed the Democratic Union for implementing the system of taxes that is now in use. No one knows who controls the influx of taxes or the reason that taxes are so high in our society. The tax situation, for example, may be completely changed by the former Communists. Finally, they were able (as they claimed) to take over Parliament and form a new coalition government. All of the parties have refused to cooperate with them, and the situation is at a stalemate.

The former Communists said that they had their representatives for a new government if the president would send a letter to other political parties and ask them to give their proposals for appointments to the new government. No one asked specifically for anyone except the former Communists and the Democratic Union, as far as I know.

The last thing I would like to point out is that this election was much more professional than the election two years ago. The candidates were more prepared and the people were more prepared for the elections, although the voter turnout was about 52 percent. I would say the voter turnout was moderate.

MR. JASIEWICZ: I appreciate your comment concerning the money situation. Indeed, the amount of money put into the election changed the outcome. Americans know that better than anyone else. I think, however, that money is just one important factor; the apparatus and the bureaucracy are also important. The importance of the bureaucracy is found particularly in the case of the Peasant Party. Its local administrative structure and management structure survived, unlike what happened to the Polish United Workers Party (now the SLD), which basically lost most of its apparatus. The SLD lost, for instance, its logistic basis—its buildings, offices, and so on. The Peasants, however, were able to preserve their logistic bases and their apparatus, people who had experience in running party affairs. From this point of view they are the best organized party in Poland. This organization contributes greatly to their success— more than money in their case.

You are right that for the Democratic Left Alliance in particular, the resources coming from business are very significant. Money coming from business was not sufficient to save the Liberals, however. The Liberal Party is really the only party representing itself as speaking for the emerging Polish capitalist class—the new Polish bourgeoisie. They had enough money to hire a public relations firm from London to run their electoral campaign. Their campaign was, according to many, very attractive and probably the most professional of all campaigns, but the Liberals, nevertheless, did not make it into Parliament. In short, money is not enough. Money plays a significant role, but it is not the single most important factor.

As far as the Right is concerned, I agree that they were not prepared for this election. This is, again, a point in favor of my argument. They were not prepared for the election, but they voted against the Suchocka government. They knew from the constitution that after the vote of no-confidence the president has two options: either to dismiss the government and ask someone else to form the government or to dissolve the Parliament. The right-wing parties first voted against the Suchocka government but were then surprised that the president dissolved the Parliament. Moreover, they did not get their act together to form a coalition to effectively contest these elections. Thus, they lost at their own request and are the only ones to be blamed for their defeat.

The issue of taxes is also a significant factor. Personal income taxes were introduced in Poland for the first time in 1992 and caused a great deal of confusion for many people. The major problem was that the state apparatus is not yet prepared to collect these taxes from both individuals and enterprises. The post-Communists said that they would improve tax collection and the flow of money to the state budget. Whether they will be able to accomplish this task remains to be seen.

QUESTION: The former Communists now hold the balance of power in Parliament. Do they have the military's backing? How much can they project themselves without the military's support?

MR. JASIEWICZ: The Communists are not in power yet. The post-Communist Party is presenting itself as a social democratic party that follows the rules of pluralistic democracy. It controls a plurality of seats in Parliament. Talks are being held concerning the new coalition government. No party can rule without forming a coalition with other parties. A coalition has not been formed yet, so today Poland's government in power is the acting government of Prime Minister Suchocka.

The question about the Communists and their link with the military in Poland is a good one. I do not want to overemphasize the fact that it was not the old Communist Party that won these elections because those people never denounced their Communist past. The resurgence of the Communist Party's nomenclatura and apparatus, particularly at the middle and even lower levels, remains a very real threat. Two weeks after the election, people who lost their jobs after the fall of the Communists are now reclaiming their jobs.

The military in Poland wants to be out of politics. It was used by the Communist leaders to crush Solidarity in 1981 and to impose martial law. From a military point of view, this operation was a success. It was organized and ran very smoothly. There was not much resistance, as Solidarity was a nonviolent movement, but the military nevertheless overcame the resistance in about a week. The 1981 operation was a disaster from a political and economic point of view, however. The military ran the country for about two years, but it did not solve any problems. It again let the Communist Party run its affairs. The military officers in Poland now want to stay out of politics. They want the army to be neutral. Moreover, while many generals as well as colonels are still in the army and are trained in the Communist military academies, very strong national-istic feelings also exist in the army. Some nationalistic parties established links to the army.

According to the Polish Constitution, the army ought to be apolitical. Some army officers ran in these elections, but they had to take unpaid leave from the army in order to run. An army officer cannot belong to a political party; thus, I do not see the possibility of a scenario like the one in Moscow. The Communists are hoping for the support of the army. In Moscow it is the other way; they have the support of the army, but I do not see any direct involvement of the army in political affairs in the foreseeable future.

QUESTION: American observers generally looked at the results with some disappointment and said that the new coalition would not bring great changes. How accurate is that assessment?

MR. JASIEWICZ: It is likely that the Democratic Left Alliance along with the Peasant Party and the Union of Labor will form a majority government in Poland. I also think it is unlikely that they will change Polish foreign and economic policies, at least at the international level. Vested interests are here to push the continuance of these kinds of policies. Their funding is coming from the most successful businessmen.

Moreover, they need some sort of legitimacy from the West. They need to legitimize themselves in the eyes of international economic organizations, such as the World Bank, and in the eyes of foreign governments, including the American government. I would see continuity here rather than any dramatic change.

If they, however, continue the current internal economic policies, what is likely to happen in my opinion is that they may alienate their own popular base. A split can also be seen between the Peasant Party and the Democratic Left Alliance. We have to remember that these two parties represent conflicting constituent interests. The peasants want price floors and protective tariffs on their products, so they are against a free market for foodstuffs. The people who depend on the state budget for their income cannot adjust to rising food prices. They have family budgets and want cheap food. A split might form because of this issue. I foresee inflation as an issue that will again hurt the party in power. Moreover, there could be a split within the Democratic Left Alliance. The post-Communist trade unions will object to any continuity in economic policies, while those leaders of the post-Communist Party who are now in business prefer continuity.

QUESTION: How do you explain Walesa's failure in judgment? He proved to be such a crafty politician over the years. How did he make that error of creating a nonparty bloc and basically not achieving what he planned?

MR. JASIEWICZ: Walesa is a great politician. He was not educated as a politician, but he has proved over the years that he is a great politician and statesman. Sometimes he sees certain developments before others see them and develops a feel for the direction in which he should go.

On the other hand, he has committed several mistakes and made some misjudgments in the past. This was a misjudgment on his part. He was hoping that the bloc would garner more support than it did. He was also hoping to form some sort of coalition. He will, I strongly believe, use this situation to his advantage. He will present the story to the public that he was right and that they would not listen to him, thus the Communists won. Now the other parties have to join and form a coalition. His position, however, is not good. First, according to the constitution, he basically controls the formation of the government. He appoints the prime minister, and there are no legal restraints on him. He may appoint a prime minister from a party that did not gain a plurality of the vote.

Second, if he appoints a prime minister who fails to get a vote of confidence in the *Sejm*, the *Sejm* would then appoint the prime minister. Walesa must accept this prime minister, but the prime minister still cannot nominate the ministers of defense, foreign affairs, and internal affairs without Walesa's consent. Walesa still has a great deal of control.

The Communists and the Peasant Party may join together, however, and they might be joined by some other minor parties. They would then have enough votes in both chambers of the Parliament to change or amend the constitution. This is a very interesting study because they may try to maneuver Walesa out of the picture. They may even attempt this move very soon.

This conclusion is probably one of the most important ones from this election. The Parliament elected about two weeks ago will very likely accept a new constitution that future parliaments would be unlikely to amend or change. I do not foresee the domination of any political party or group of parties in the future that will be strong enough to amend a constitution acceptable to this Parliament. Let's hope that they write a good constitution.

NARRATOR: Thank you, Professor Jasiewicz, for this most informative discussion on the recent elections in Poland.

IV.

POLISH-AMERICAN RELATIONS IN THE 1990s

CHAPTER SIX

Polish-American Relations in the 1990s: Historical Background and New Perspectives*

BOGUSŁAW W. WINID

NARRATOR: It is important that we not only see issues from our standpoint but that we put ourselves in the shoes of other leaders and citizens who may view their relationships with us in similar but also at times in differing ways. Dr. Bogusław Winid of the Polish Embassy in Washington, D.C., will guide us today in this endeavor.

Dr. Winid majored in history at Warsaw University. He received his master of arts degree in 1984 and wrote a thesis on the Crimean War. Dr. Winid continued his education by earning a doctorate in history at Warsaw University, and wrote his dissertation entitled "Polish Diplomacy and the United States of America: 1919-1939." After receiving his doctorate degree, he participated in the Diplomat Training Program at Stanford University's Hoover Institution. Earlier, he had served as a junior research associate and then research associate at Warsaw University's American Studies Center. From 1988-1989 he was a visiting scholar at the Polish Studies Center at Indiana University. We are privileged to have Dr. Winid with us.

MR. WINID: I would like to divide my lecture into two parts. First, I will discuss some of the most important aspects of Polish-

---

Presented in a Forum at the Miller Center of Public Affairs on 24 February 1994.

American relations during the interwar period, from 1919 to 1939. Then I will move to the most recent developments, especially concerning Polish attitudes toward NATO membership and the Partnership for Peace (PFP) initiative. I will begin with a discussion of the main framework of Polish-American relations during those years.

After Poland regained its independence in 1918, many groups within Polish society expressed a need for assistance from the United States. Ignacy Paderewski was one of the main proponents of this idea. Paderewski's activities on behalf of Poland during the war as well as statements made by President Woodrow Wilson led Poland to believe that America would offer it free foodstuffs and support Polish territorial claims at the Paris Peace Conference. The first activities of the newly organized Polish diplomatic service were aimed in this direction. In the middle of 1919, however, it was discovered that some of these assumptions were inaccurate. Polish policymakers regarded the Paris Peace Conference results as favorable to Poland only to a limited extent. Paderewski's compromises were interpreted by some as evidence of his weaknesses and an incorrect evaluation of the country's actual capacities. Nevertheless, Paderewski's pro-American orientation ensured that Poland would make use of all of the types of cooperation that the United States could offer. This orientation brought good results in my opinion, and the criticisms of Paderewski have little support in historical analyses.

During the period of Paderewski's prime ministership, a plan was developed that emphasized the significance of American political and financial assistance in the struggle against the territorial claims of Poland's unfriendly neighbors. Paderewski was trying to present Poland as a crucial factor to European stability. He hoped, thereby, to attract the attention and support of Washington. At the end of 1919, however, Americans began to evaluate the situation in East Central Europe from the perspective of future relations with Germany and Soviet Russia rather than with Poland. Thus, Paderewski's and his followers' efforts, unfortunately, had only limited results, as demonstrated by America's limited support for Poland during the Polish-Soviet war of 1920. Polish-

American relations from 1921 until 1924 were much less intensive than before.

The next change in the direction of Polish diplomacy toward the United States took place in the middle of 1924. This change was caused by America's new policy toward Europe and the country's economic problems. After adoption of the Dawes Plan in 1924, the U.S. State Department and the leading American financial and industrial corporations took active part in the European stabilization. This move created new possibilities for Poland.

A policy geared toward American-oriented diplomacy was implemented by Prime Minister Władysław Grabski and especially by his foreign minister, Count Alexander Skrzyński, who later succeeded him as prime minister. Skrzyński was able to affix his own foreign policy to the framework of international relations outlined by President Calvin Coolidge. The major Polish diplomatic achievement in regard to relations with the United States was negotiating the Stabilization Plan and Loan of 1927. (Unfortunately, when the loan was finally signed, Skrzyński was no longer in power. Beginning in 1926, Józef Piłsudski controlled the Polish government.) The Stabilization Plan and Loan Agreement gave Poland more than $72 million, which at that time was a huge amount of money for the Polish economy.

This positive change in political relations regrettably never found another fruitful follower. After Piłsudski's coup d'etat in 1926, diplomacy toward the United States was carried out with greater reserve, and after 1929, the Great Depression reduced financial and trade contacts. The expectations of Polish policymakers and the country's economic elites were thus never realized.

Abandonment of the political line of Paderewski and Skrzyński facilitated the goals of German and Soviet propaganda in the United States. After World War I, the German revisionist campaign in the United States was much more efficient than Polish counterattempts. As a result, in the early 1930s, Secretary of State Henry Stimson regarded Poland as a country totally dependent on France and pushed for territorial changes in the so-called Corridor region in Pomerania as an antidote to the social and political dissatisfaction and economic crisis in Germany. Naturally, Polish diplomacy was openly opposed to giving any territory back to Germany.

Franklin Delano Roosevelt's election as president in 1932 initially did not significantly change American attitudes toward Europe. The main problem for Polish diplomacy was the gradual change of FDR's views on Germany and Russia. The tensions in American-German relations after Hitler came to power were favorable for Poland. Politicians no longer mentioned changing borders.

On the other hand, Roosevelt extended U.S. relations with the Soviet Union, and this change was to have serious consequences for Poland in the future, especially during World War II and at the Yalta and Teheran Conferences. Actually, the real roots of Yalta in Roosevelt's philosophy are already visible in the 1930s. At the same time, Polish diplomatic efforts concerning relations with the United States weakened overall. Both Józef Piłsudski and Foreign Minister Józef Beck were convinced that the United States was playing only a minor role in European diplomacy and therefore underestimated the importance of Polish-American relations. For example, Beck declined an invitation for an official visit to the United States in 1936 and again in 1937. Essentially, Polish diplomacy in the interwar period did not fully use its possibilities of generating interest in Poland to gain political allies in the United States.

Other nonpolitical factors were also operating against Poland. Solving economic problems was a high priority. Warsaw authorities initially failed to appreciate the real and potential links between American businesses and policy-making institutions. Polish diplomats preferred to concentrate on purely political issues and make economics subservient to politics, as was common in traditional 19th-century diplomacy. They understood only with difficulty and after some passage of time that American priorities were to some extent the reverse of Polish values and priorities. For American politicians, economic concerns shaped policy rather than the other way around. This difference created an additional difficulty for Polish diplomacy. The only solution was domestic economic development. For the relatively weak Polish economy, cooperation with the United States was a double-edged proposition. On one side, the influx of new technologies, management methods, and capital could stimulate the country's economic development. Moreover, American capital was regarded as politically neutral, which, for example, eliminated a consideration of state security. At the same time, American investment in Poland could have become a political asset as a symbol of American support, a prospect that Paderewski and Skrzyński had wanted to encourage.

On the other side, increased economic contacts with the United States could become dangerous for the budgetary balance. The overall balance of trade in terms of volume was unfavorable for Poland. In practice, it would have meant a flow of hard currency out of Poland, running from a few million to tens of millions of dollars—a huge sum for the Polish budget. No free market methods to reduce the trade deficit with the United States existed. The majority of Polish products were of lower quality than American ones, with high transportation costs and customs duties further reducing the attractiveness of Polish export goods in the United States. The successful exportation of ham and other meat products to the United States in the mid-1930s finally marked the breakthrough in bilateral trade. Nevertheless, this single instance of success could not significantly reduce the large trade deficit. For this reason, practically all Polish governments, regardless of their political orientations, used administrative methods to restrict imports from the United States. To further curb the flow of hard currency from the country, even the activities of American banks and shipping lines were occasionally restricted.

All instances of government intervention were viewed extremely negatively by Washington authorities, which was no surprise. These interventions also harmed cooperation in other fields. During practically all negotiations, the United States insisted on removing trade barriers as the main condition for future talks. No Polish government would agree to this condition. They feared an even larger deficit and flooding of the Polish market by cheaper American products, which would in turn undercut domestic producers. During the whole interwar period, it was therefore impossible to reach a sensible compromise. Polish-American economic relations remained underdeveloped. This lack of agreement, of course, had a negative effect on diplomatic contacts and had some serious political side effects. American corporations and banks preferred to invest in German or even Soviet markets where profitable opportunities were more numerous.

The American opinion of Polish economic development changed only slightly in the late 1930s. Most Americans continued to view Poland as associated with intolerance or internal tensions. Exaggerated accounts of Poland's economic problems in the American press served to confirm these negative stereotypes. Despite numerous efforts on the part of Polish diplomacy, these negative feelings never fully disappeared. Polish efforts did not manage to convince Americans that the prosperity of Poland was essential to the maintenance of overall European stability. One of the most significant results of these problems was the conduct of American diplomacy during the Second World War. Practically from the beginning, FDR looked at Poland as a part of the Soviet sphere of influence. To some extent, this perception and the results of the Teheran and Yalta conferences were rooted in the lack of cooperation in the 1930s. Poland was occupied by the Soviet army at the conclusion of the war, and the future Polish Communist government was created first in Chełm and then moved to Lublin in 1944.

People should not forget that for about four years there was a civil war in Poland. It was, of course, a hopeless struggle. Poland was unable to change the line of history. From 1945 to 1989 it is difficult to talk about Polish-American relations or about Polish diplomacy toward the United States because everything was directed from Moscow. That overriding situation makes it difficult to define a distinct Polish foreign policy during that time. As the first non-Communist foreign minister, Krzysztof Skubiszewski, stated, Polish diplomacy with some exceptions was not working to achieve national assets but rather was working toward the interests of the so-called Socialist Commonwealth or, more directly, Soviet imperial interests.

This situation existed until the collapse of communism in Poland in 1989. When the first non-Communist government by Prime Minister Tadeusz Mazowiecki was organized, Krzysztof Skubiszewski was nominated as the minister of foreign affairs. His nomination was the beginning of a process implemented to create a new independent Polish foreign policy.

The Polish government quite quickly decided that the main goal for Polish foreign policy would be integration with the NATO Alliance and the European Community. Poland would like to be a member of the family of European nations again and become an active member of the Euro-Atlantic strategic organization—NATO. According to Polish evaluation, NATO still has a very strong role for the future. The Alliance not only stopped Soviet aggression but also stabilized the situation on the whole continent. In terms of security and stability, however, there is still much to do in Europe.

The visible lack of security poses a threat to the success of economic and political transformation in Central Europe and creates one of the impediments to more vigorous American investment in that region. The admission of Poland, Hungary, the Czech Republic, and Slovakia to NATO will liquidate a potentially dangerous security gray zone in Central Europe that, unfortunately, some countries can consider as their sphere of influence. It will not create a new division of Europe; to the contrary, it will close the unfortunate division of Europe created by the Yalta Agreements, the 50th anniversary of which has just passed.

The unstable situation in the former Soviet Union and potential imperial ambitions of some countries in that region constitute a threat to Poland's security and the security of all of Central Europe. The enlargement of NATO will bring a zone of stability and security closer to the Russian border and will prove that countries emerging from communism and implementing rapid transformation processes can and will be welcomed into the Euro-Atlantic Community.

The United States was, is, and will be the leading member of the NATO Alliance. Its position on such issues as the admission of new members should direct the debate on the timetable and method for implementation. As a superpower, America can effectively influence other members and introduce practical solutions and ways to absorb Central European countries into NATO.

As we can now see, in the beginning two approaches toward Poland's membership in NATO were competing in the Clinton administration. The first one concentrated mostly on the Partnership for Peace (PFP) idea. The second one proposed more concrete measures—associate membership or something like a 10-year track for full membership.

The Polish government was in favor of more concrete and precise policy, but the administration chose the Partnership for Peace approach, which entails a looser structure. Poland has just recently accepted the basic terms of the PFP. In our view, PFP clearly increases Polish security. It confirms American commitment to Europe, which from the Polish viewpoint is significant for the continent's security and stability. It partially opens the Alliance to the East and thus makes Polish hopes of joining Western security institutions more realistic. In addition, PFP provides for greater quality and quantity of military contacts with NATO, adjustment of our armed forces to meet Western standards, and consequently, mutual interpretability. It also gives Poland the right to consult with NATO when a crisis arises. Finally, PFP strengthens the commitment of all of the partner countries in Central and Eastern Europe to the preservation of democratic societies, maintenance of the principles of international law, civil rights, tolerance, and so on.

The Partnership for Peace program now needs to fulfill its general framework with a more detailed agreement and concrete action. Two aspects of this process are of particular relevance to Poland. First, countries like Poland that feel strongly about joining NATO should be provided with the particular criteria for membership and the time frame for the process. Clear assurance is needed that, as the *Washington Post* editorial puts it, "States meeting agreed standards of democratic competence and matters of fitness can accept NATO membership in a specific time." Such an assurance should be given not mainly to satisfy the aspirations of these nations, but also to recognize their importance for the stability and security of the United States, NATO, and Europe.

Statements have been made by President Clinton and Vice President Gore linking the security of Central and Eastern Europe with that of the United States. According to the American United Nations ambassador, Madeline Albright, during her trip to Poland, "The security of this region is of direct and material importance for the security of the United States." This statement and others like it help to dispel some of the growing apprehension in Central Europe that this region has been assigned a different role. These countries also receive a commitment to the security of Central Europe as an indication of American interest in that region. The United States will now be asked to make good on its commitment in practice by ensuring that Poland and other Visegrad countries are actively involved in Partnership for Peace and that they will in the future be able to obtain NATO membership.

Some problems exist, however, especially from an economic point of view. Poland needs additional funds to finance membership. The government has declared that it is ready to shift the budget so that some funds are directed to PFP activities and programs. While money is important, Poland will not allow it to become an impediment to Euro-Atlantic security. There are hopes that Poland will receive some assistance from the United States, especially for the standardization of military equipment, which is a necessary first step in developing a higher level of cooperation and military compatibility. Also, hopes are high that Polish-made products will be able to compete on a normal basis for contracts to supply the United States and other NATO forces with goods and services.

Such contracts could help in the export and import of defense-related equipment. There is no secret that this issue is of great importance to Poland. Polish defense manufacturers are in a crisis, and Poland is experiencing high unemployment and an inadequate use of resources.

PFP is an attempt to build a Europe without competing countries or groups driven by ideological, nationalistic, or historical lines of division. It is also an attempt to make use of the unique opportunity provided by the collapse of communism and an apparent consensus among European nations that national development should emphasize democracy, rule of law, private ownership, and openness with the world. It is difficult not to share this ambition. Indeed, it would be an unforgivable mistake not to take advantage of such an opportunity.

These are the reasons why Poland supports PFP as an initiative that, while not corresponding fully to Poland's aspirations and sense of urgency, could provide a more comprehensive and visible response to the Polish quest for security. Yet, what if there is no chance for a Europe without alliances? If there is no consensus on democracy, if ideological, nationalistic, or historical considerations take precedence over human rights, prosperity for individuals, and respect for neighbors, what can be done? How should we respond?

These questions, of course, cannot be definitively answered. The answers are conditioned on many circumstances—some universal, some local. What is clearly necessary, however, is a close monitoring of each European country as it handles its internal situation and external obligations. Only through such a process can European security and stability be maintained and Partnership for Peace achieve its aims.

Poland's main goal is to be a full member of NATO, and it is looking at Partnership for Peace as a track that will lead it to NATO, not one that will take it backwards. On the Polish side, we will try to be active and maximize the opportunities that PFP offers to Poland. Poland is ready to commit the necessary resources to fulfil the obligations and accept the responsibilities of NATO membership. Poland is committed to implementing infrastructure development activities that will facilitate its participation in and its support for NATO military activities. When President Clinton visits Poland in July of this year, we hope to be able to go forward with negotiations and move further toward our goals.

QUESTION: How many Russian troops are currently on Polish soil? Second, do you think the results of the recent Polish elections will make a difference in the Partnership for Peace negotiations between Poland and the United States?

MR. WINID: To answer your first question, there are no Russian troops in Poland. The last ones returned to Russia in September 1993.

To answer your second question, I am certain that the elections will not affect PFP negotiations. Based on our constitution, President Lech Walesa is responsible for foreign relations, the military, and internal ministries, so the key decisions in foreign policy are in his hands. President Walesa has guaranteed that Poland will continue on the PFP path and all of the leaders of the parties that won in the parliamentary elections have openly supported NATO membership. I do not foresee any changes.

QUESTION: What is the current status of the Polish military forces?

MR. WINID: In the Polish army, the number of troops is declining. The budget is a big problem—allocations for the military get smaller every year. As far as I know, the military has some reserves that are now being used, but the general trend is to cut military spending. As I mentioned previously, Poland will nevertheless have some special funds assigned for NATO integration purposes. The size of our military is defined by the Vienna Convention that dictated limits on armed forces for each European country. In most categories Poland is currently just below the limits. Poland does not have funds, for example, for more than 100 helicopters. In fact, it has about 40 or 50. This level represents restructuring of our military, a task that requires a great deal of money. Unfortunately, the economy is not producing enough funds to move quickly, but Poland is moving in the right direction. These problems will be visible—there is no question about that.

QUESTION: In recent years, questions have arisen in the United States concerning the degree to which the government represents the people. In Poland, does a disparity exist between the views of the government and the people, particularly regarding economic policy? Is there wide divergence among the views of the people themselves?

MR. WINID: The elections last September were the third after the fall of communism, so I think people were educated on how to vote and how democracy works. In this sense, I do not see big differences between the views of the government and the people.

The one important factor in the last elections was the new electoral system, which changed the results in the sense that some powerful groups are no longer represented in the Parliament. The system requires parties running as a coalition to reach an 8 percent threshold of votes nationwide, and single parties to reach a 5 percent threshold. Unfortunately, practically all of the center and right-wing parties were running separately. They were not able to form a coalition, which was a sad mistake. The left-wing parties were able to unite before the elections and run as a coalition. Therefore, some big and influential groups are not represented in the Parliament.

A good test of the popularity of the different parties will be the local elections taking place in May and June 1994 and the next presidential election in 1995.

Regarding the economic situation and the attitudes of the people, I would argue that to change the system back to the socialist model is impossible. It is also impossible to change the direction of the Polish economy. We went too far to go back. Some people who had privileges during the Communist era, however, were hurt by the transition, as were a large part of Polish society. Local governments no longer guarantee the complete medical services or social security networks that existed during Communist rule. I personally believe that the role of the state is not to guarantee everyone universal medical treatment, and the state should not be taking care of citizens from the time they are in nursery school until retirement. About 20 percent of the populace, however, a very solid electorate for left-wing parties, does believe in that sort of system. They are mostly from the older generation. Most of the members of the younger generation will benefit from these freedoms and are in favor of them.

QUESTION: Is there a risk that Russia may try to get Poland in its sphere of influence and dominate it economically and politically?

MR. WINID: Unfortunately, such a risk exists. Russia will probably not be able to use its economy as a tool to control Poland. Poland redirected its foreign trade to the West, so it is not totally dependent on the Russian market. The only thing Poland currently imports from Russia in large amounts is natural gas—about 80 percent of the Polish supply comes from Russia. This reliance is important, but most of Poland's gasoline comes from the West or the Middle East. Total economic domination by Russia is therefore unlikely.

Russia could try to dominate Poland politically, but without help from Western Europe this scenario is highly unlikely. In reference to recent developments in Russia and the tremendous success of Vladmir Zhirinovsky and his party, if he is taken seriously, it should be noted that his first goal is the Indian Ocean. If I am not mistaken, he wants to go to the south and not to the west. I do not know where Alaska is on his priority list.

QUESTION: What role, if any, did the United States play in the victory of Solidarity over communism?

MR. WINID: I think it played quite an important role. This was particularly true with President Ronald Reagan. He was one of the first presidents of the United States who clearly defined the Soviet Union as the "evil empire," and though many arguments have been made about the value of his approach, I believe it was important that he portrayed situations as right or wrong and not as a gray area. Moral issues were important in dealing with a country like the Soviet Union. Reagan's hard approach toward the Soviet Union was very helpful from the Polish point of view and made him very popular in Poland.

QUESTION: How much did Dr. Zbigniew Brzezinski contribute to the transformation of Poland from communism to democracy? Do you recall any incidents in which he shaped policy?

MR. WINID: I was a little too young to personally remember when Brzezinski and Carter visited Poland. There is no question of Brzezinski's popularity in Poland. During the first presidential elections, some rumors circulated that Brzezinski should run for the presidency. He declined and said he was not confident enough about the internal politics of Poland to run for the presidency. I argue that he would have achieved good results in such an election. He might not have won against Walesa, but he would have had a solid block of support.

Brzezinski's books, writings, and attitudes toward the Soviet Union were a positive influence. Most of his writings were translated from English into Polish, so they have been available to the general public in Poland. We can only admire his writing. I recommend the latest edition of *Foreign Affairs*, which will be published at the end of March. It contains an article by Dr.

Brzezinski on American policy toward Russia and American-Russian relations entitled "The Premature Partnership." I think it is an extremely accurate and significant piece of work.

QUESTION: What industries in Poland, including shipbuilding and coal mining, are contributing, if at all, to Polish unemployment?

MR. WINID: Unfortunately, Poland's unemployment is relatively high. Last year the unemployment rate in Poland was 16 percent. There is some discussion as to whether this figure represents real unemployment, because Poland still has a gray zone in its economy in which people prefer to hire someone illegally and therefore avoid paying taxes for that worker. From a budgetary point of view, this attitude is very negative.

Poland also has many problems with so-called local unemployment, especially in the small cities. For example, one big factory, which is involved in an industry currently in decline, may employ practically the entire town. Some regions thus have extremely high unemployment because of this one state-owned enterprise. Such a factory does not have a chance at privatization because of its weaknesses. Meanwhile, no other local industries exist that could absorb the people fired or laid off from this big state enterprise.

Shipyards are currently in good shape because the shipping industry is booming again. They have full investor portfolios, and most of them are now privatized. The big shipyard in Szczecin was privatized, and the privatization of a shipyard in Gdansk is proceeding. This area is thus definitely not the main problem.

The mining industry is a problem because during the Communist era, it was heavily subsidized by the government, and naturally miners and their trade unions are now demanding that the subsidies continue and actually be increased. It is difficult for the government to find the money to subsidize even agriculture, but the trade unions, especially in Silesia, are so powerful that the question becomes very important. No matter what government is in Warsaw, it will have to deal with this difficult situation.

Poland was trying to restructure parts of the mining industry, but none of it paid well. The situation in Poland is definitely unlike Great Britain, where Prime Minister Margaret Thatcher had enough power to just close down the inefficient mines. This scenario will not occur in Poland because of the weakness of the government and the lack of resources.

The best answer to all of these problems is privatization, which is moving ahead, although sometimes too slowly. In the reprivatization of lands, buildings, and industries, the problem of what should be returned to the previous owners arises. This situation is a legal nightmare. These properties changed hands very often—someone bought it from the state, or perhaps someone bought it from other citizens. I do not know the best answer, but the Parliament must find a solution. My personal view is that Poland should reprivatize everything as soon as possible and return as much property as is feasible.

For example, consider the problem of a big building in Warsaw that was previously owned by a single individual. Currently about 100 people live there. This building is subsidized by the local government. If this building is returned to its previous owner, he or she will clearly demand market rates. This fee is the owner's right, of course, but then these 100 people would be against this reprivatization move. This type of situation is dangerous also from the political point of view, because it is easy to find someone who would use such circumstances to argue for keeping the socialist system. There is no easy answer to these questions.

QUESTION: You mentioned that Roosevelt's willingness to consign Poland to the Russian sphere of influence dated from the early 1930s. What might have been the sources of that attitude?

MR. WINID: What I said was that Roosevelt's pro-Soviet approach was visible in the beginning of the 1930s. The first incident is Roosevelt's handling of the official diplomatic recognition of the Soviet Union in 1933 and the way Roosevelt handled this official diplomatic recognition. All of the Republican administrations before FDR—Harding, Coolidge, and Hoover—were strongly against any contacts with the Soviet Union. Questions still remained about American-owned property in the Soviet Union confiscated by the Communists. When Roosevelt became president, he did not use the State Department or the Treasury Department for negotiations;

117

rather, he used his personal envoys to make a deal with Soviet Foreign Minister Maxim Litvinov. The result of this deal was that the Soviets did not give anything back—a good deal for them.

The 1930s contain many other examples of Roosevelt's attitude toward Russia. For example, the Roosevelt administration credited most American exports to Russia. Even a 10 percent credit, however, was impossible to arrange for Poland. In 1938, Roosevelt tried to sell the Soviet Union a battleship with all of the modern equipment. This sale was stopped by the U.S. Department of Defense.

Lend-Lease was given to Stalin without a single question or rule concerning how it was to be used or any questions about the Molotov-Ribbentrop Pact of August 1939. Stalin clearly said that he expected Poland's borders to be those dictated in this pact. At the Teheran Conference, Roosevelt openly told Stalin that all arrangements concerning Poland should be made after the November elections of 1944 because of Polish-American voters, but he had no objection to accepting the borders in the Molotov-Ribbentrop Pact. He then agreed not only on this line, but also to the creation of a so-called Soviet-friendly government in Poland. In fact, it meant a Communist government.

NARRATOR: The last question leads to the subject that we hope you will discuss the next time you visit, and that is the subject of whether there is any alternative for Poland, which has suffered four tragic partitions and is caught between Germany and Russia. Belgium and the Netherlands, in an earlier period of history, were caught in the path of German invasion. They were given security guarantees and, in a sense, a kind of neutral status. When we think of the tragedy of Poland, we always ask the question, Is there any alternative? We leave that as the next subject we hope you will discuss with us.

V.

POLAND'S NATIONAL SECURITY PROGRAM

CHAPTER SEVEN

Updating the Transformation Process in Poland*

MACIEJ KOZLOWSKI

NARRATOR: This month has been a historic one for Poland. On 1 August 1994, a significant event occurred: the 50th anniversary of the 1944 Warsaw Uprising against Nazi occupation. For 63 days the Polish partisans of the underground Home Army sought to drive the Nazis from the capitol as the Soviets, who had encouraged this resistance, stood by and did nothing to assist Polish forces. The Soviets not only did nothing, but they also failed to respond to the American offer to provide assistance. The anniversary was commemorated with Russian and German representation. German President Roman Herzog expressed his grief at the action taken against the Poles. The significance of the Warsaw Uprising is that it highlights both the enormous courage and bravery of the Polish people and also some of the tragic events that have occurred in Polish history. With this event and the relatively recent ending of the long Soviet domination of Poland in mind, it is important to update the continuing transformation process in Poland as well as Poland's national security problems.

We are privileged to have Minister Counsellor Maciej Kozlowski, the deputy chief of mission at the Polish Embassy in Washington, D.C., speak here today. He is a historian, columnist, translator, author, and diplomat. He was a distinguished member of the Polish democratic opposition during the Communist regime.

Presented in a Forum at the Miller Center of Public Affairs on 16 August 1994.

Minister Kozlowski was also a member of the editorial board of the *Tygodnik Powszechny*, a weekly publication that became a home for the democratic opposition and also a place for foreign statesmen, politicians, journalists, and the opposition to meet. Throughout this period, Minister Kozlowski traveled around the world to speak and explain to the world what the opposition was attempting to do in Poland.

He holds both master's and doctorate degrees and has taught at several universities, including Jagiellonion University and the underground Solidarity University. He was also editor-in-chief of a Solidarity daily paper in Kraków, *Wiadomosci Krakówskie*. In 1969 he was sentenced to a five-year prison term for smuggling political literature into Poland but was released after two-and-a-half years. Minister Kozlowski has been a frequent guest speaker at American and European universities, and his awards include the Nelly Strug Award for the best history book published in Poland in 1986, the Solidarity Award for the collection of historical essays, "Landscapes Before Battle" (1986), and the Polish Underground Union of Journalists Award for preserving honesty in journalism. We are pleased to welcome him back to the Miller Center to hear his perspective on Poland's transformation.

MR. KOZLOWSKI: I was last here in the Miller Center two-and-a-half years ago. The situation in Poland was then quite different, so this is a good time to update what is happening in Poland, East Central Europe, and the whole region. It has not lost its importance in the last few years, although the thrill of transformation is over. Poland and other Central and Eastern European countries are less often in the headlines. Other parts of the world now receive more attention, although the problems and the importance of this part of the world have not diminished but are actually increasing with the transformation in progress. This process of deep political and economic transformation is happening not in only a few countries, as was the case two or three years ago, but in the entire region. Most important, the transformation is occurring on a psychological level.

I will first provide a brief picture of what is happening in Poland. As mentioned, Poland recently commemorated the 50-year anniversary of the Warsaw Uprising. It is a part of World War II history less well known outside of Poland; for Poles it has tremendous importance because it was the most tragic of all Polish national uprisings. In less than two months, 200,000 people were killed and Warsaw, the capitol of Poland, was totally destroyed. Those losses were a very heavy price for Poland to pay at the end of World War II, and that event shaped Poland's national psychology. This is why Poles attach such a great importance to this anniversary.

With the deep political wisdom of Poland's president, Lech Walesa, and some of his advisers, it was decided to turn this event into an international event of reconciliation rather than just a national commemoration. This event was in deep contrast to the events two months earlier in Normandy, wherein only the victorious allies celebrated D-Day. Despite the fact that the Warsaw Uprising was a lost battle, Poland was courageous enough to invite not only its historical allies—the presidents of France and the United States and the prime minister of Britain—but also its adversaries, the presidents of Germany and Russia. The term *adversary* is used because although Russia formally was an ally, in practice the relationship was adversarial in the sense that the Warsaw Uprising was watched with cold calculation by the Russian army. By not helping the Home Army, the Russians killed the possibility of an independent Poland opposing Russia after the war.

Not everyone could attend the commemoration, but the most important visitor, the new president of Germany, Roman Herzog, did attend. It was a controversial moment, and many Poles were not happy about it. They said it was still painful to invite a German when Germany was heavily responsible for what had happened. Political wisdom nevertheless prevailed, and Mr. Herzog did a splendid job. He made a historic speech in which he stated that he understood the feelings of those who were unwelcoming to him but that he came in the name of Germany to apologize for all that was done by Germany to the Polish nation. These words represented a historic healing of Polish-German relations in conjunction with the famous kneeling of Chancellor Willy Brandt in front of the Warsaw Ghetto monument in December 1970. Such actions constitute the bridge over that vast chasm between Poles and Germans created during World War II. Without Polish-German reconciliation, there will be no true and lasting peace in Europe. Franco-German reconciliation was crucial to organizing the Western European Union (WEU) and the European Community (EC). Now, moves to enlarge the EC by pushing it to the East, which is a goal for Poles and Germans, would not be possible without sincere reconciliation between these two nations. President Walesa's invitation to President Herzog and President Herzog's words of apology, which touched Polish hearts, represent a historic moment. Both countries made a big step toward a united Europe and helped remove the old division between East and West.

This August anniversary also brings us to the problem of security because, in addition to President Herzog, Russian President Boris Yeltsin was invited. Contrary to President Herzog, President Yeltsin declined the invitation under the poor excuse that it was sent too late and he was too busy. In a situation such as the reconciliation of two nations, there is nothing that is more important. Yeltsin did send his chief of staff, Sergei Filatov, and a low-level delegation. American President Bill Clinton could not come because he had been in Warsaw three weeks earlier, but Vice President Al Gore came to represent the United States. British Prime Minister John Major also came. French President Francois Mitterrand could not come, but he was quite sick following a cancer operation.

Mr. Filatov, who is personally very friendly toward Poland, nevertheless gave an unpleasant speech without any kind of apology for what happened 50 years ago and with no attempt to feel with those who were remembering the loss of Poland's capitol. While this anniversary was a big step in the reconciliation between Poland and Germany, it did nothing to bring Poles and Russians closer together. This is an important factor in the future of Europe's security system.

The security situation in Europe is unclear. On one hand, Europe has a well-established and well-organized alliance of 17 countries—the North Atlantic Treaty Organization. On the other hand, Europe has Russia, which is the inheritor of the Soviet Union not only diplomatically as a member of the U.N. Security Council but also militarily as a superpower with the largest army in the world—over one million people—and a vast nuclear arsenal. Furthermore, Russia is not hiding its will to reestablish some kind of influence over the countries that broke away from the former Soviet Union or, to be more precise and more historical, from the Russian Empire, noting that the Soviet Union was an inheritor of the Russian Empire that lasted much longer than the 70 years of the Soviet Union. The breakdown of this empire was the most crucial moment in history for many centuries. The question is, Will this breakdown have a lasting effect or will this situation exist for just a short period? Will the Russian Empire reappear in another form? These are the most important questions currently facing politicians, political scientists, and historians in this transition period. The Russian Empire, in one way or another, formed the history of the world in the last few hundred years. The question is now open as to whether history will continue to be shaped by this empire.

Some forces are working toward rebuilding the empire. The best example is Belarus, a country that simply does not want to lead its own existence but would prefer to come back under the umbrella of Russia both economically and politically. On the other hand, Ukraine is independently minded but in a deep economic crisis. No one knows if without true reforms Ukraine can sustain its independence relative to Russia, which is reforming itself. While Russia has many problems and setbacks, progress in political and economic reform is now visible, in contrast to two years ago when reform was a very distant possibility. Russia is ready to embrace the free market. Yet, the market is not functioning well, and many problems such as the criminal elements still exist. Russia reached the point of no return a couple of years ago, and they can only go forward into the free market.

This progress, however, is not irreversible. It is unlikely that Russian would turn back, but a reversal to totalitarian rule and a more imperialistically minded Russia is feasible. That fear prompts Poland's strong desire to join the Western security structures. It is not that Poland currently fears Russia and therefore wants NATO to deliver Poland from Russia. Poland still hopes that it will not have to fear Russia, that Russia will transform itself and become a more democratic and open society, for open and democratic societies usually are not threatening to their neighbors.

Poland nevertheless cannot live in this precarious part of Europe without an insurance policy. Poland's development will be hampered without such security because it will have to consider any economic, political, or social decision in the context of a possible future threat. Therefore, Poland's membership in Western European structures, including the European Union (EU) and the WEU, can give Poland both economic prospects and the feeling of security. The fact that Poland wants to join NATO is obvious; Poland makes a great deal of noise sometimes. Some people say it makes too much noise, but in this world where everyone looks out for his or her own interests, if one does not make noise, no one will pay attention. Making noise in this case is absolutely necessary.

Poland is trying to explain that its membership in NATO is in the best interest of NATO itself. The best security instruments are those which do not need to be used. NATO was successful because it never had to fight. The greatest success of NATO was that it was so powerful, no one dared attack it. That fact was the best proof that it was a successful military alliance.

Security problems arise when there is a gap, a grey zone, or a piece of unattended real estate. That problem is exactly the current condition in Europe. NATO is on one side and Russia is on the other. In between, a gray zone exists. With unattended property, someone is always thinking about taking advantage of the situation. Russia is now too weak and has too many problems. But if such a gray zone exists, it tempts. This situation is a security threat.

The world should be organized in such a way that there are no places where someone would be tempted to take advantage of a potential weakness. Approximately 60 wars have occurred in the last 60 years all over the world, but only two were really world wars, both of which started on Polish soil. The geographic position of Poland makes it strategically important because it is between East and West, and there is always a temptation to enlarge a sphere of influence over territories in the heart of Europe by one party or another. Safely putting Poland in one place would therefore provide much more security for all parties concerned, not only Poland.

Imagine the following scenario. Some nationalistic tendencies win in Russia, and there is perhaps a desire not to directly attack Poland but to try to influence Poland. Poland then opposes Russian actions, and the possibility of a much bigger conflagration than Bosnia emerges. The world now has a war situation. The West or NATO becomes involved; they cannot just let it go. Such a scenario can be prevented. If NATO provides security, there will be no temptation for this type of action.

Many arguments are circulating against Poland's membership in NATO. Some of these points are valid, but some are quite superficial. One of the superficial arguments is that the West cannot do anything to jeopardize the transformation process in Russia. Poland's position, however, is that by bringing Poland closer to NATO, Russia's transformation is not jeopardized, but enhanced. Leaving Poland in this gray zone is what truly jeopardizes the situation because Russia itself is debating what to do in the future and what Russia will be. Those questions pose a serious problem because Russians themselves do not know exactly where Russia ends and who Russians actually are. As the historical nucleus of an empire, Russia does not have clearly outlined borders. Is Chechnya part of Russia or not? Is Georgia part of Russia or not? Georgia may be an independent country belonging to the United Nations, but what about the Russians living there? They do not feel Georgian; they feel Russian. The people of Russia have to do some soul-searching to finally decide who they are and what their role in the world order will be. Nevertheless, as long as this unclear security situation exists, there will always be a temptation to try to roll back the Russian empire. Poland was part of that empire for nearly 200 years and an independent state for only 20 years. Poland was part of the empire under czarist times; it was part of the empire under Soviet times. In addition, Russians still think of Poland as a country that should be in one way or another connected with Russia. This kind of thinking is dangerous. Until Russia has no illusions about Poland's independence, the possibility exists that this situation might be repeated. This internal debate will be painful, but it will be healthy for Russia.

This situation is similar to the history of Algeria and France. In the 1960s, a debate arose in France about what to do with

Algeria. France was fighting a very nasty war to keep Algeria French, many French people could not imagine France without Algeria. French President Charles de Gaulle was wise enough to cap this kind of thinking, and now no one thinks of Algeria as rightfully a part of France. The same is true of India and Britain. For many Britons in the last century, India was a part of the British Empire, and people could not imagine Britain without India. Leaving an empire is a painful process, but the sooner and more clearly it is done, the healthier it is for the country leaving.

Good arguments do exist against Poland's membership in NATO, namely, that it is best if no new lines are drawn in Europe. Poland's situation is common to many other countries. Hungary, Bulgaria, Romania, Albania, Ukraine, Georgia, and many others are in a similar security situation relative to Russia. If Poland is admitted to NATO soon and these countries are not, they will be furious. They are feeling insecure. Poland certainly understands this problem, and therefore Poland also understands that the expansion of NATO must be a gradual process. Poland is the most prepared to enter NATO, but Poland hopes that the other countries will go through their transformation and finally be ready to enter NATO as well. It is difficult to say when these countries will be ready because the process of transformation is up to each individual country and their citizens. Each country must decide the pace at which it will proceed.

Herein lies Poland's main point of controversy with the Clinton administration. Of course Poland does not believe that Russia will eventually be a part of NATO. It does not say that openly and formally, but NATO with Russia would not be an alliance that could exist. One alliance cannot have two competitive superpowers with nuclear weapons because that type of competition would blow up any structure. NATO is not strong enough to accommodate two nuclear superpowers. One is enough. I therefore do not believe that Russia will be able to join NATO. Once Poland is part of NATO, however, some kind of strategic understanding should be reached between Russia and an enlarged NATO. Some kind of a dialogue and close cooperation should be initiated as well. Poland does not expect Russia necessarily to be a threat. It hopes that Russia will not be one.

There is a perception that Poles in particular have an anti-Russian sentiment and therefore should not be allowed to join NATO because they will poison NATO with their anti-Russian phobia. That perception is false. There is no anti-Russian feeling in Poland. Poland has a strong political disagreement with Russia. It has a very strong difference of opinion on security structures, but in Polish history that kind of ethnic hatred, for instance, that exists between Serbs and Croatians in the former Yugoslavia or between Jews and Arabs never existed.

Russians are generally well liked in Poland. For example, in the last couple of years millions of Russians have visited Poland. Some also come to trade or work in the black market. Every day about 30,000 citizens of the former Soviet Union cross Polish borders, staying different lengths of time. Usually about one to two million Russians are visiting Poland at any one point in time. In the four years since the frontiers opened, not a single incident of hate-crime has occurred against a Russian in Poland. The same is true for Poles in Russia. Russians also do not hate Poles, and many Poles are visiting Russia. Furthermore, Russian culture is extremely popular in Poland. The most read authors in Poland are Dostoyevsky and Tolstoy. Russian music and cinema are very much cherished. There are intermarriages between Poles and Russians.

Poles say that they like Russians unless they are in uniform and marching together. Poles oppose Russian imperialism, but they like Russians as people. This situation gives Poles and Russians hope for the future. Reconciliation between Poland and Germany has occurred despite previous ethnic hatred. It was possible to overcome such hatred. The western frontier between Poland and Germany is now the friendliest frontier that Poland has, and approximately three billion marks are left by German tourists in Poland. While Poland has a deficit in its balance of payment in trade, it also has an enormous surplus of foreign reserves because of Germans coming to Poland. This tourism is not only good for Poland's economy, but it helps to build bridges between the two countries.

These same bridges can be built with Russia, but only if Russia forgets about the possibility of subdividing Poland. It is only possible to build truly good relations with Russia when Poland is secure in the Western alliance. Good relations between Poland and Russia are not only in the interests of Poles and Russians, but also in the much broader interests of the general security in Central Europe, the whole of Europe, and the world. Unfortunately, when trouble starts in Central Europe, it has a tendency to spill over into other areas.

QUESTION: How much concern exists in Poland about the nuclear material remaining in Russia and the surrounding countries?

MR. KOZLOWSKI: In Poland there is less concern than in the United States for several reasons. First, Poland has been living in the shadow of these nuclear materials for nearly 40 years. They have basically gotten used to it. Second, Poland has many more immediate concerns. The Russian army left Poland in September 1993. When there was an attempted coup in Moscow, that was an immediate threat. That possibility was more of a threat than this nuclear threat.

Third, Poland is more concerned not with the material in the hands of the military, but with these unsafe nuclear power plants. Poles still remember the 1986 Chernobyl nuclear accident. It deeply affected Poland, and the possibility of something like that happening again is a real concern. When the plant in Chernobyl was dismantled, that was the best news Poland could have received. Nonetheless, a whole chain of these unsafe nuclear power plants exists, in Latvia and Ukraine, for example.

QUESTION: You give a favorable impression of German-Polish relations and of the prospects for their future relations remaining peaceful. Do you foresee any adverse effects on this relationship from the German minority still left in Poland and from the organizations that members of this minority have formed, some of which are revisionist in nature, such as the East Prussian Wolves? Do they have the potential to upset German-Polish relations in the future?

MR. KOZLOWSKI: The potential of upsetting a peaceful relationship always exists, and history teaches that no state can be secure

130

forever. Some possibility of tension always exists. This frontier between Poland and Germany is settled for now, but that settlement does not mean there are not anti-Polish feelings in Germany. Some cases of Poles being beaten in Germany have occurred. An ultra-nationalistic movement in Germany is creating tensions.

Fortunately, Poles understand what is emerging, and the mainstream in Germany is strongly opposing this movement. The same ultra-nationalist movement exists in Poland. Two German drivers were even killed in Poland two years ago. That incident was a hate crime against the Germans; however, no such hate crimes against Russians have occurred.

In reference to the German minority, Poland is fortunate that it has a very homogeneous society. Of the people inhabiting Poland, 98 percent are Poles, and thus the German minority is small. Therefore, Poland can give them all possible rights without feeling threatened. The German minority can have its own schools and newspapers. Poland even adjusted its electoral law so that minorities have a better chance to get representation in Parliament than under the normal proportional representation system. As a result, Poland has four members of the German minority in the lower house of Parliament and one member in the upper house.

The German minority in Poland is generally loyal. There are, however, some possible tensions, stemming mainly from Germany's greater degree of wealth. Germany provides some assistance to the German minority in Poland, while people of Polish origin receive no such assistance. Fortunately, these tensions have not yet gotten out of hand, but such a possibility always exists. Some opportunistic politician might like to exploit natural controversies, and a band of such people can really turn human minds upside down, as in the former Yugoslavia. People were living together peacefully for centuries, and now they are killing each other simply because some people fueled this hatred. Until now there has been no such tendency on the German or Polish sides. In addition, the enormous amount of trade between these two states is so important to many people that there is a strong tendency to keep German-Polish relations in good standing. When avenues for trade are opened, it is then more difficult to foment hatred.

QUESTION: The United States is decreasingly interested in European security—not in terms of NATO but in terms of taking on additional commitments. This emerging French-German-Polish relationship of military exercises, military training, and so forth will de facto create a security community perhaps stronger than that implied by simply signing on as a NATO member. NATO, therefore, may not have the significance that it had before 1989. Given this situation, is it really NATO membership that will provide security for Poland, or is it the quality of the relationships that Poland is able to forge with its Western neighbors that will achieve this goal?

MR. KOZLOWSKI: I disagree with your assertion that NATO was successful in a given set of circumstances in which it can no longer be successful. It is a logical question—if not NATO, then what? NATO exists. It is good, common wisdom that if something is proven useful, let it continue. If NATO is dismantled, a new situation would be created that would be even less stable than the current situation with NATO.

Apart from NATO's role as a counterweight to the Warsaw Pact, it also created stability among its members, a very important achievement. NATO was the institution that finally changed Germany. It is a great historic achievement to change Germany from an aggressive power into a benevolent player among equals in Europe. Germany is now a model democracy and plays according to rules. It is the most stable country in Europe, and this status is to a great extent because of NATO and its membership in NATO.

Another example of NATO's success in keeping peace and stability among neighbors is Greece and Turkey. I am absolutely certain that if it were not for NATO, a shooting war between Greece and Turkey would have occurred at some point. Their controversies, however, never went beyond the shouting match stage because they are both NATO members.

NATO brought its member countries together in the sense that now any kind of warfare between them is unthinkable. Psychologically, because of the past 40 years of coexistence in common security structures, these countries cannot fight each other. Even those countries that have fought each other in the past could not

132

imagine doing so again. For instance, France and England had a 300-year history of wars between them.

Poland would like to join the community wherein that kind of chemistry exists. In this area, NATO has still a useful role to play. It can also provide Poland with security in the sense of an insurance policy. No one knows what will happen in Russia. Often in history when a country has serious internal problems, it tries to attack someone else because that outside threat brings internal unity and serves to explain the hardships the population has faced. Outside threats strengthen the holders of political power. The possibility that internal problems could be so exploited by Russia cannot be excluded. In such a case, NATO serves as an insurance policy against Russia's crossing that frontier.

QUESTION: What is your view of the European Union? Why does Poland aspire to be a part of NATO rather than possibly the European Union?

MR. KOZLOWSKI: Poland is aspiring to be a member of both organizations. It has a long road to follow to join the European Union; it is now an associate member of the EU and is strongly demanding some kind of set timetable for full membership. Joining NATO and the EU are treated by Poland as two parallel processes. It is technically easier to join NATO than the European Union because to join NATO all one has to do is upgrade one's military, increase compatibility, rearrange the chain of command, and so forth.

In order to join the European Union, Poland has to adjust its entire economy with inflation still growing about 30 percent a year and an agricultural system that employs around 30 percent of the labor force. Poland is not yet ready to join the European Union; its economy cannot compete with the rest of the EU. Poland has a per capita income of between $3,000 and $6,000 a year (depending on how it is measured), while in most of the Western European countries GDP per capita averaged approximately $15,000 a year in the early 1990s. Poland therefore still has a long distance to go, and it takes time. Joining NATO may only take from one to two years. Poland feels that after it joins NATO, it will be easier to join the European Union. Poland now has a proposal to join the EU politically (sort of like being a member of a political club) and have a much longer period for full membership economically.

QUESTION: Was any comment sought from Russian President Yeltsin's nemesis during the 50th anniversary that was so important in Poland? Was any kind of comment or note received? Did he not attend, or was he not invited?

MR. KOZLOWSKI: In terms of Yeltsin's nemesis, one may think of Vladimir Zhirinovsky, the ultra-nationalist. His star is waning. He was kind of crazy and did not last long in the spotlight.

Alexander Rutskoi is a different story. He was released from prison after being cleared of charges of participating in the October 1993 antigovernment riots. He is now a private citizen, although he still claims to be Russia's vice president. I do not know if he had any comment about Poland's anniversary celebration. Some comments appeared in the Russian press, and they were very unpleasant. They basically said that Poland was forgetting who the real oppressors were. The understanding and feeling is still widespread in Russia that Poland and all of Eastern Europe were liberated by the Russians from Nazi occupation. One can call it liberation, or one can call it changing from one occupation to another. It is simply a question of how one looks at it. That question is the main historic problem between the Poles and Russians. How should the last 50 years be viewed? Were these years an occupation or a price Poles paid for liberation? Russia feels no responsibility for not aiding the Polish resistance during the Warsaw Uprising. Russians believe in the Stalinist line that the offensive had to stop because the lines were overstretched and that it had nothing to do with politics. Everyone now knows from many sources that these claims were false, but that kind of reading of history is still widespread in Russia.

NARRATOR: As Minister Kozlowski goes back to Poland, we want to wish him well, and we shall watch his future career with great interest and great pride in having known him. Thank you, Minister Kozlowski, for this illuminating discussion.

VI.

DEVELOPMENTS
IN THE MID–1990s

CHAPTER EIGHT

Recent Developments in Poland*

GIFFORD D. MALONE AND CLAY L. WIRT

NARRATOR: We are pleased to have Gifford Malone and Clay Wirt return to the Miller Center to tell us about recent developments in Poland since their last visit in April 1992.

MR. MALONE: Looking back over the last five-and-a-half years, Poland has had a record of quite remarkable progress. Considering the problems it has had to confront, five-and-a-half years is not a long time. When the economic reforms went into effect in January 1990, the real changes began. At the same time, despite the progress achieved so far, many problems certainly remain.

When the reforms began, Poland had what economists call a negative rate of growth. This past year, by contrast, Poland had one of the highest growth rates in Europe. Gross domestic product (GDP) increased 5 percent this year. It increased about 4.5 percent last year, and outside observers predict that this trend will continue for at least the next couple of years.

The other interesting point is that the private sector contribution to GDP in Poland is around 56 percent according to official statistics, although it may actually be higher. Such a high contribution from the private sector is quite an achievement, especially when one recognizes that the privatization program (i.e., privatization of state enterprises) that Poland put into effect has gone much slower than planned for several reasons, mostly political.

Presented in a Forum at the Miller Center of Public Affairs on 6 June 1995.

There is still quite a long way to go on that front. While the politicians have worried about that problem and tried to solve it one way or another, the private sector has nevertheless continued to grow on its own at an amazing rate.

Poland does have a very high unemployment rate. It was, officially, 16 percent in 1994. While it is not the highest rate in Europe (the Spanish and Irish rates are both higher), it is not satisfactory either. Most people in Poland, whether they are liberal or conservative in their outlook, believe that the unemployment rate is actually lower. Unemployment is measured in Poland by the number of people who have registered as unemployed, but the so-called gray market is very active. A certain proportion of these technically unemployed people are making money on the side. This figure therefore probably suggests that economic conditions are worse than they are. The latest figure put unemployment at just over 15 percent, so the trend is probably more positive.

Polish exports are doing well. The deficit is under control, and the standard of living is rising. Again, however, one must be careful with the statistics. Soon after the economic reforms went into effect, the standard of living supposedly dropped 40 percent. What did that imply? I was not sure.

I went back to Poland for the first time after about 16 years in June 1990, and I wondered what the many noticeable changes meant for the standard of living. Warsaw did look rather drab and rundown to me. For the first time, however, I found myself in the middle of a traffic jam in Poland. Also, while goods were priced much lower under the Communist system, few goods then were actually available. In contrast, for the last several years, people have been able to buy anything in Poland, if they can afford it. My current impression is that the standard of living is certainly rising, although the inequalities of wealth that are likewise developing are somewhat disturbing. This change means that some people, particularly those on pensions, are not benefiting as much as one would hope from what has occurred.

Agriculture is very important for Poland, although Americans do not read much about it in U.S. newspapers. Forty percent of the Polish population lives in rural areas, 27 percent of the work force is engaged directly in agriculture, and a larger proportion of the work force is engaged in occupations related to agriculture. It is therefore an important part of the country and the economy.

Poland was unique in the Communist period in that most of its agriculture remained private. Throughout the Communist years the individual Polish farmer stood as a bulwark of individualism against the state—a significant symbol. At the same time, however, the farmers were dependent upon the state's centralized command economy, and they have benefited less from the economic developments of the last several years than various other segments of the population. In the early stages of the economic transformation, their living standards clearly declined. They no longer had guaranteed fixed prices, and competition from abroad rose dramatically. The situation was not one in which they could find immediate benefit, and this fact was reflected in the makeup of the last Polish government, whose prime minister was from the Peasant Party (PSL).

Farmers' dissatisfaction with their situation was clearly one of the reasons the Peasant Party did so well in the last parliamentary elections in October 1993. Waldemar Pawlak, who was chosen as prime minister and served until February 1995, pursued policies in the last year and a half that did benefit the farmers. Economists can argue whether they were sensible policies; they tended to perpetuate the subsidy situation in Polish agriculture, which is not tenable over the long term. Poland has many small farms—a million Polish farms are under five hectars in size (about 12 acres)—and therefore individual productivity is low. Many people in farming must have an additional form of employment to make a living, but there is considerable overpopulation in rural areas. This situation will have to change in the long term. I do not mean to suggest that Polish agriculture is in a crisis or that the Polish farmers are in a crisis. They clearly are not, but over the long term any Polish government will have to face the problem of what to do with the large rural population.

There are other problems in Poland as well. For instance, Poland does not have the kind of labor mobility that Americans enjoy. Therefore, when a state-owned factory upon which one town is dependent closes, those people cannot merely move somewhere else where there is work. One of the reasons for that problem is the housing situation, which, as in all post-Communist countries, is very poor. A consistent theme of Communist rule in every formerly Communist country was that housing was allowed to deteriorate dreadfully. As a result, there simply is not enough housing now in Poland. Whenever I go back to Poland, I see houses being built in the countryside. My impression, however, is that these homes are for the wealthy, or at least the relatively wealthy. That type of construction does not solve the problem of what happens to the unemployed worker who is looking for a job some-where else.

Problems with the banking system still exist. These problems also relate to the housing situation. Poles cannot simply go out and get a mortgage for 7 percent. It is more likely to cost about 45 percent; therefore, most people do not borrow money. Lending for businesses is similarly handicapped, although progress is being made on that front.

Poland is still working on the infrastructure upon which a modern economy depends. Some recent figures indicate that apart from Albania, Poland still has the smallest number of telephone lines per person of any country in Central and Eastern Europe. Russia and even Bulgaria have more telephone lines per person. I am unclear on exactly why this situation exists, but it is an example of the fact that Poland has much work to do on its infrastructure.

The issue of decentralization of government, a controversy that started quite soon after the Mazowiecki government came to power in 1989, is another significant issue in Poland's progress. Local government has been reenergized in Poland. Elected local governments did not exist in the past, and in the early days of the post-Communist period a whole range of new local governments were elected for the first time. More recently, the Pawlak government (in power from October 1993 to February 1995) was not in favor of decentralization, which led to problems on that front.

One of the things that has struck me continuously during my visits to Poland is the extent of entrepreneurial spirit and enthusiasm the Polish people have displayed for doing things in new ways. It is really quite striking. I am referring generally to those people 40 to 45 years old and younger. The younger generation is extremely impressive in its attitudes and abilities, which is another hopeful sign for the country. If anyone had asked me 20 years ago when I was living in Poland under the Communist system whether the spirit of entrepreneurship would take hold, I would have been skeptical, and I would have been wrong. Attitudinal differences certainly exist between the generations; older people tend to be less satisfied with what is happening now. I think that these differences are natural, however.

Turning to the question of politics, if Poland is making progress, how does one explain the fact that the Poles could elect a government of former Communists? This phenomenon is not limited to Poland. A number of former Soviet bloc countries have elected governments led by former Communists. The standard explanations for this occurrence are weariness, frustration, and the electorate's nostalgia for the old times. The situation is not that simple, though. I do question, at least in the case of Poland, the notion of nostalgia. Although Poles do want some of the benefits that they used to receive and the kind of security that was provided for them, I have the sense, and others share this view, that no one is looking for the return of communism or the command economy. Harvard economist Jeffrey Sachs, who did some work in Poland in the early 1990s, has said that the controversy really boils down to interest groups. The farming sector and those people over 45 years old are responsible for bringing these former Communists back to power, according to Sachs. This evaluation does have some credibility. The Polish population did not grow very fast in the later Communist years, and pensioners make up 32 percent of the adult population in Poland, as compared to 21 percent in the United States. People on disability comprise 9 percent of the adult population, although this figure includes rather generous definitions of disability. In addition, many people have taken early retirement in Poland as a result of the process of downsizing some of the large state-owned enterprises.

The question of party organization is also important. The Communists were always well organized, and their organization remained in place despite the changes. The other parties were new, and they did not have time to build the kind of networks that are needed. These differences also played a role in the elections. Ironically, the electoral law changes put into effect before the present government came to power magnified the former Communists' victory. Before the parliamentary elections in October 1993 there were 29 parties in the Polish Parliament. Everyone agreed that this situation made it difficult to get any business done. As a result, Parliament passed a law that required parties to receive a minimum of 5 percent of the votes before they could attain representation. Coalitions were required to obtain 8 percent of the votes. Ultimately, most of the parties could not clear that hurdle. Therefore, in the redistribution of seats, according to a formula upon which all of the parties elected to Parliament before October 1993 had agreed prior to this latest election, the leading parties got proportionately more seats than their popular mandate required. Thus, the former Communists, known as the Democratic Left Alliance (SLD), and the Peasant Party were able to form a governing coalition with a substantial majority.

On the other hand, one has to keep a certain sense of perspective when examining this situation. Only 52 percent of the people voted in the last election. Of that 52 percent, 20.4 percent voted for the former Communists. One can argue, as I have heard some Poles do, that those results mean that the present post-Communist government represents only 10 percent of the electorate. Those figures can be debated, but what this statistic does mean is that a huge surge of support for the former Communist groups does not exist.

In practice, there has been an uneasy coalition of the former Communists and the Peasant Party since those elections. Their views are not the same on some rather important issues. Curiously, these former Communists claim to be, and in most cases actually are, wedded to the development of a market economy. Many of them are now capitalists; they took advantage of the changing situation. The Peasant Party has paid lip service to that idea, but its leadership is not as wedded to the market economy as the others. Since the elections, there have been many disagreements between the two parties. The result was that in February 1995, due in large part to maneuvering by President Lech Walesa, Waldemar Pawlak resigned and a former Communist, Józef Oleksy, became prime minister. It is too soon to see exactly what he will do. The latest public opinion poll on the parties showed that the former Communists had 25 percent support, the peasants had 18 percent, and the Union of Freedom, which represents the old Mazowiecki group, had 18 percent.

Polish politics is currently dominated by the upcoming presidential elections in November 1995. Not all of the candidates have yet been chosen. There is no limit on the number of people who can run, but the major candidates are known. One of them will be Aleksander Kwasniewski, the leader of the Democratic Left Alliance. The people I talk to seem to believe that he will be one of the top candidates in what will probably be a runoff election. The Poles have a system of presidential elections like the French system: If no candidate gets a majority, there is a runoff between the top two. One recent poll on this subject shows Kwasniewski and Jacek Kurón, who is from the Union of Freedom, running more or less neck and neck, with other candidates not doing so well. President Walesa has amazingly low public-opinion poll ratings. In this particular poll he had 10 percent of the support, but as people keep saying about Walesa, one can never count him out of the race.

Taking a longer view of this situation, the post-Communist issue is not really the most important issue in Poland's political evolution. I think the Poles will work through that phase, and noting that the former Communists are thus far in favor of a market economy and even support Poland's entry into NATO, the differences are not as extreme as one might think from reading American newspapers. This system, however, is still under construction. Poland must still pass a new constitution. Currently, seven drafts of this constitution are under examination, and they are quite different. One of the key issues concerns what kind of presidency Poland will have—one similar to the French model, which has a strong president, or the German model, which has a ceremonial president. The parties themselves are still trying to decide what they should do and how they should behave. They are also trying, fairly unsuccessfully, to adopt a spirit of compromise and accommodation so they can get together and form workable coalitions. This political system is really a work in progress, and although I am dwelling on the issues that pose problems for Poland now, I am not really pessimistic about the future.

On the economic front, despite the problems and deficiencies, considerable progress has been made and the major changes that have occurred are irreversible; the direction has been set. Unless the political leadership blunders badly, the private sector will continue to grow in the next few years, and political and economic problems will work themselves out.

On that note, I would like to say a few words about the American Committee for Aid to Poland. The committee has had two primary purposes. From the beginning, it has tried to facilitate the work of American nonprofit organizations in Poland, helping them make contacts and educating them about the Polish scene. It also has tried to strengthen the rapidly expanding nongovernmental, noncommercial sector within Poland itself. This NGO sector has developed with great speed; there are now between 10,000 and 20,000 nongovernmental organizations in Poland, and they are certainly one of the building blocks for democracy and the development of a civil society.

There is still much to do, but a great deal of progress has been made. The committee, according to plans laid out several years ago, will be dissolved at the end of this year. We believe that it has completed its initial mission, which was to help others get started in Poland. USAID is now actively involved in Poland, and dozens of other American organizations are working there now.

MR. WIRT: I will cover two areas: first, the effort of Virginia local government managers to serve as partners and mentors to Polish local government managers, and second, some of the challenges and problems in Polish local government. Like Mr. Malone, I have a positive outlook in the long run for local governments in Poland. It is my privilege now to have visited Poland five times to work with local governments, and I will soon return.

The program that I am involved in is called Managers to Managers. While the term *city manager* is well known in the United States, it is new to Poland. Thus, for purposes of our program, the term *manager* refers to the mayor or deputy mayor or people with significant administrative responsibilities, at least to the level of department head. In this hands-on exchange program, a Virginia manager travels to Poland and spend two weeks working with a Polish local government manager. The same Polish manager will then come to the United States and spend a month working alongside his Virginia counterpart. As of this fall, over 50 internships will have taken place under the Managers to Managers program.

The Center for Public Service at the University of Virginia also has a program called the Senior Executive Institute (SEI). The Institute's annual two-week senior executive program for city managers is well known around the United States as a premier program for professional training. We are pleased that SEI has dedicated a slot to a Polish manager participating in the Managers to Managers program. The participating Polish manager who was here last year from Olsztyn, Poland, said that it was far and away the most outstanding professional experience that he had ever had.

The momentum for the Managers to Managers program came from my meeting the vice president of Warsaw in April 1991 at a working group meeting of the Metropolitan Governance Program of the United Nations. This Polish official asked me to try to bring together local government managers in Virginia to help local government managerial officials in Poland deal with management and reform issues in the transition to democracy.

Although the Managers to Managers program was not initiated by government funding, it has received three $60,000 grants from the United States Information Agency (USIA). Furthermore, the Metropolitan Governance Program of the United Nations recently sent someone to Poland to observe and write a case study of the program. This observer reported that despite differences in cultural, political, and social backgrounds, Managers to Managers has produced effective results based on friendships that would not have been possible with one-time consultations. Due to the long-term duration of these contacts and the program's informal nature, Managers to Managers is able to adapt to the specific needs and interests of the participants.

The program has addressed a number of subject areas that are largely determined by recommendations from the cities involved. In Poznan, city development—including investment promotion, city marketing, and small business support—has been the focus for the last two years. Additionally, Fairfax County, Virginia, and Poznan are exploring formal cooperation in the area of economic development and trade. Work is even underway on a three-way relationship that would include Moscow.

In Opole, Managers to Managers has dealt with the organization of city hall, citizen information and participation programs, and public schools, pairing Opole's officials with their counterparts in Roanoke, Virginia. As an outgrowth of this contact, Opole and Roanoke County signed cooperation agreements with the original solidarity-led city council and again with the new council headed by the former Communists.

In Warsaw, the program has focused on economic development and financial issues, while the city has also been instrumental in translating a number of documents into Polish that are used in Virginia's local governments. In Kraków last summer, the program focused on management of public housing and local budgeting. This year it focused on helping the city analyze potential development of public-private partnerships for revitalization and development in the area immediate to the Kraków train station. Due to the historical nature of the downtown portion of Kraków, this area is one of the few where development is still allowable. In Olsztyn, the focus has been on economic development and general management issues.

Three years ago management issues such as organizing the manager's office and dealing with staff were predominant. These kinds of management issues still arise, but other areas, particularly those focusing on how the local government relates to and can be more supportive of the market economy, are now at the forefront.

One of the primary challenges and problems currently faced by Polish local governments and officials is, as Mr. Malone mentioned, the stalling of reform. From the standpoint of a number of local officials, reform is not merely stalling; it is treading backward, at least from the perspective of those from the larger or midsize cities. The smaller communities and the rural areas may have a somewhat different perspective.

When the Local Government Act of 1990 was passed, it was considered to be a promising first step, but it was envisioned as only a first step. Other steps were to follow. Those steps were supposed to transfer to local governments significant added responsibilities and local revenue powers, but they have not been taken. Although some responsibilities have been transferred, the central government continues to tell local governments how they have to carry out these responsibilities. The central government also has not given the necessary taxing power to fulfill these duties; rather, the central government provides the money in the form of grants. The actions of the central government are thus not completing the reform that was anticipated, and they run contrary to the expectations of the reform movement.

In addition, whereas in Parliament the former Communist Party and the Peasant Party are in power, the post-Solidarity forces won in local elections last year in some of the larger cities such as Kraków and Poznan. Some of those officials are still in favor of the more far-reaching kinds of reforms that the country began after the fall of communism. The fact that these reforms have not been fulfilled is a source of frustration, leaving the feeling that the cities are not able to do things as effectively or efficiently as they feel they could.

It is important to note, however, that based on the program's work in Opole, the former Communists now in leadership positions in some of these midsize cities may also be very interested in continued reform. They like the idea of decentralization of power. They see the merits of conducting government locally, and they do not like unfunded central government mandates. Thus, the change to the post-Communist prime minister that Mr. Malone mentioned could possibly signal new reforms that would affect local governments—a good sign. The people, however, are not very optimistic. They have to see something actually happen.

One example of the stalling of reform concerns the percentage of government money that comes from local revenues. Three years ago it was 17 percent, and today it is 15 percent. Local governments now have more responsibilities, yet they have a smaller piece of the overall ability to raise local revenues.

Some "positive signs" regarding the long-term future of Polish local government can nevertheless be seen. I would like to mention a few, as I have a positive outlook in the long run for the local governments. In 1992, I was concerned about the lack of root democracy, good management skills, and so forth. These concerns are still valid, but Polish cities now have five years of experience under their belts. Slowly but surely a success story is developing. It is not so much an issue of how fast they move; it is that they get pointed in the right direction.

Local governments are proving to be very stable institutions. They have consistently received good ratings in the public opinion polls, ratings that have even gradually risen. The functioning of the city councils also show signs that local governments are improving. These councils are very large—up to 45 people in some of the larger cities. Instead of having people on these councils who basically stand on a belief and are adverse to compromise, more pragmatism is beginning to predominate. People are increasingly willing to work through compromises.

Another problem has been the initial tendency of newly elected city council members to think that they have the right to manage everything, resulting in a great deal of micromanagement. Now, however, the hiring of appropriate staff and the delegation of certain management responsibilities is increasing. The city councils are beginning to spend more time on policy and letting the staff be more involved in management.

An additional good sign is that while little can be done at present by local governments to raise revenue or convince the central government in Warsaw to relinquish some of the power it still holds, local governments can work on several other issues. For example, they can do something about their own expenditures; they can work on the formulation of their local budget and accountability of funds. These types of reform are starting to occur, and Kraków in particular has taken the lead. As local governments become better organized, they will be in a much better position to convince banks to discuss with them the potential for long-term financing, such as bonds, that will help the local governments address the critical infrastructure problems they face.

QUESTION: Is the sort of cooperation that exists between Virginians and Poles something that is happening throughout the United States, or is Virginia a unique example?

MR. WIRT: The manager association program is unique to Virginia because it is the only one of its kind in the country. There are good reasons for linkage between Virginia and Poland. They have many things in common—most notably, a love for democracy.

QUESTION: Are exchanges between Virginia and Poland being made in other areas?

MR. WIRT: School systems are also conducting exchanges. The first exchange involved school superintendents. I expect others will follow. Even though the manager exchange program is unique from Virginia's standpoint, many other groups in the United States, Austria, and the European Union are linked with Poland. As Mr. Malone told me back in 1991, the need in Poland is great enough that there should be no fear of duplication. Because Poland is starting from scratch, there is a need for input from a variety of sources and countries. I cannot speak for the school exchanges, but I suspect that at the local government level, Poland wants to model itself on France, particularly in the budgeting area. In other areas, local governments want to model themselves on other systems, such as those in the United States or Austria. The important thing from the Managers to Managers program's standpoint is that the American participants are not there to tell the Polish participants what to do. We are there to share from our many years of experience of managing local governments in a democratic society. The Poles have to make their decisions based on their own culture and interests.

LADY BLANKA ROSENSTIEL: One of the gentlemen from Opole we hosted last year, who was here for the second time, said he had learned so many wonderful things in America. When he returned to Poland, he wanted to apply his knowledge to Polish city management, but he had a lot of opposition because the other people were not exposed to certain ideas. They sometimes did not even know what he was talking about. Could video tapes be sent to all of the people in the city governments so that they could discuss these ideas?

MR. WIRT: Referring to Opole specifically, the program did send the video tape of its training session last summer to that city so that the newly elected people could have the benefit of watching it. That is one area in which the program could get better results. There is much room for improvement in being able to provide that sort of support.

MR. MALONE: This problem is a generic one. I have been involved with many groups that are training people in the nonprofit sector of Poland. One person is trained and returns to Poland, but no one else in that person's organization has any frame of reference. The person who has been trained brings back all sorts of new ideas, many of which are greeted with skepticism because no one else has had the same experience. One of the frequent recommendations I hear now is that these programs should never train just one individual; they should train at least two or three from the same organization so that they are mutually supportive when they return and begin to introduce new ideas.

MR. WIRT: Obviously, we have never conducted this sort of program before, so we are also learning these things. When the program began, to maintain continuity, we decided to continually train in the same cities. In most of these cities, exchanges have now occurred for three years, and most of the exchanges include participation of two Polish managers.

MR. MALONE: When these exchange programs began, American organizations went to Poland, conducted short training courses, and then left. It was not very effective, at least not as effective as it could have been. It is important, as is being done in Mr. Wirt's project, to keep the relationship going and have follow-up sessions to establish these relationships. It makes a huge difference.

NARRATOR: We have had a wonderful discussion. It is good to hear of the encouraging steps being taken to assist Poland during its time of difficult adjustments. We appreciate Mr. Malone and Mr. Wirt sharing their knowledge of the problems that need to be addressed and the efforts being made to improve Poland's economy and government. We also thank Lady Blanka Rosenstiel for introducing us to the challenges and opportunities of Poland.